SPEAK EASY
EFFECTIVE COMMUNICATION SKILLS TRAINING

Perfect Your Speaking, Listening & Connection Skills In Just 7 Days

Copyright © 2024 by LearnWell Books.

All rights reserved. No part of this publication may be reproduced, distributed, or transmitted in any form or by any means, including photocopying, recording, or other electronic or mechanical methods, without the prior written permission of the publisher, except in the case of brief quotations embodied in critical reviews and certain other noncommercial uses permitted by copyright law.

References to historical events, real people, or real places are often fictitious. In such cases, the names, characters, and places are products of the author's imagination. We do this where it's important to protect the privacy of people, places, and things.

689 Burke Rd
Camberwell Victoria 3124
Australia

www.LearnWellBooks.com

We're led by God. Our business is also committed to supporting kids' charities. At the time of printing, we have donated well over $100,000 to enable mentoring services for underprivileged children. By choosing our books, you are helping children who desperately need it. Thank you.

This Is Really Important.
It's a Sincere Thank You.

My name is Wayne, the founder of LearnWell.

My Dad put a book in my hands when I was 13. It was written by Zig Ziglar and it changed the course of my life. Since then, it's been books that have helped me get over breakups, learn how to be a good friend, study the lives of good people and books have been the source of my persistence through some pretty challenging times.

My purpose is now to return the favor. To create books that might be the turning point in the lives of people around the world, just like they've been for me. It's enough to almost bring me to tears to think of you holding this book, seeking information and wisdom from something that I've helped to create. I'm moved in a way that I can't fully explain.

We're a small and 'beyond-enthusiastic' team here at LearnWell. We're writers, editors, researchers, designers, formatters (oh ... and a bookkeeper!) who take your decision to learn with us incredibly seriously. We consider it a privilege to be part of your learning journey. Thank you for allowing us to join you.

If there's anything we did really well, anything we messed up, or anything AT ALL that we could do better, would you please write to us and tell us (like, right now!) We would love to hear from you!

readers@learnwellbooks.com

We're sending you our thanks, our love and our very best wishes.

Wayne

and the team at LearnWell Books.

WELCOME TO OUR COMMUNITY

"It's like a private online book club"

 Imagine if you could actually meet and talk with other readers of this book and share your experiences.

 Imagine if you could chat with the author or join them on a live Q&A!

 Imagine getting access to the author's notes and other exclusive, unpublished material.

You can do all of that and a lot more in the LearnWell Online Community!!

→ Download your **Workbook**
→ Chat directly with the author!
→ Meet and feel supported by other readers and their experiences.
→ Access additional, exclusive content about this topic and others.
→ Join our live Author Q&A sessions online.
→ Learn faster, make lasting changes, and have 10 times more fun!

This is part of our commitment to creating the best learning resources in the world.

Scan the QR code to get FREE access
www.learnwellbooks.com/talk

To you, my dear friend,

You have the most amazing things to say
that no one will ever hear
until you learn to speak.

CONTENTS

Introduction — 11

PART 1: THE FOUNDATIONS OF EFFECTIVE COMMUNICATION — 15

1. The Qualities Of An Effective Communicator — 16
   An Introduction To Effective Communication And Connection

2. Why People Who Communicate Effectively Always Win — 25
   The Truth About Effective Communicators And Why Motive Matters

3. How YOU Can Communicate Effectively — 36
   Unlocking Your Potential To Connect And Find Success

PART 2: TRAITS OF AN EFFECTIVE COMMUNICATOR — 43

4. Start With You — 44
   Developing Self-Awareness For A Complete Transformation

5	**Without This, You Are Irrelevant** The Power Of Empathy And How To Build It	54
6	**The Reason For 90% Of Your Success In Communication** The Words People Use Matter Far Less Than Everything Else	64
7	**How To Shape Your Attitude** The Power Of A Positive Attitude And How To Adopt One	84
8	**A Rare And Highly Valuable Skill** The Impact Of Great Listening Skills And How To Listen Effectively	96
9	**3 Habitual Approaches You Need** How To Reestablish Your Passion For Life And Prioritize Joy	110
10	**A Foundation Of Confidence** How To Build Confidence From The Ground Up	117
11	**Laughter & Smiles** Going The Extra Mile With An Effective Sense Of Humor	133

PART 3 YOUR CONNECTED LIFE — 145

12 Nailing The Greeting — 146
Why A Good Greating Is Your Greatest Advantage And How To Execute One

13 Memorable Interactions — 158
How To Ensure Every Conversation Leaves The Most Positive Impression

14 Socially Aware & Tactfully Brilliant — 177
Applying Your Effective Communication Skills In Real Time

15 Building Strong Relationships — 189
How To Apply Effective Communication Skills To Various Professional And Personal Relationships

Conclusion — 205

References — 206

YOUR WORKBOOK

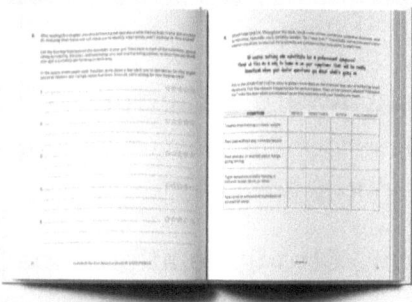

A shocking truth was discovered by a study done in 1987 – **people only remember 10% of what they read!**

That seems so discouraging.

But here's the **GOOD NEWS** – reading is **NEVER** a waste of time. As long as you do **one** important thing …

The same study (by National Training Laboratories) shows that you will remember 90% of what you read when you **put your new knowledge into action**!

Here at LearnWell, we aim to create **the world's best learning resources**. So, we have included a highly engaging **Workbook** that helps you put your new knowledge into fun, practical action.

So, make sure you download your **FREE Workbook**. You'll find it located inside the **LearnWell Community**. Simply scan the QR code below for access.

Get your Workbook in the LearnWell Community
Scan the QR Code for access or go to:
www.learnwellbooks.com/talk

INTRODUCTION

Humanity needs people like you. The ones curious to learn more and adapt to new information. It needs people willing to let go of old perceptions and aspects of themselves in order to grow, shift, and transform. It needs people who stand like solid old houses, stabilized by good bones and years of weathering change. It needs people with the drive to get the best out of life and the willingness to share their joy with others.

Humanity needs people who can *connect*. The ones who glow and hold space for a more loving, society. It yearns for more compassion, camaraderie, and hope. It's desperate for those who light up rooms, engage conference halls, and speak with unwavering self-confidence.

Humanity needs this book.

But before you continue, forget what you know about charisma and communication – or at least put it aside for the moment. Become open to a new perspective. Allow the information you find here to refresh you, remind you, and change you. Let it prove why becoming an effective communicator will change your life.

This book comprises 3 parts, carefully curated to help you understand, acquire, and practice effective communication. The 3 parts include:

PART 1: THE FOUNDATIONS OF EFFECTIVE COMMUNICATION

A section dedicated to understanding effective communication, including what it is and what it definitely isn't. Here you will find stories, lessons, and the inspiration to embrace it for yourself. After all, you're here because you want to create a better life for yourself. This section shows you why and how effective communication will get you everything you're looking to attract. It's here to prepare you and get you excited for the brilliant future ahead of you.

PART 2: TRAITS OF AN EFFECTIVE COMMUNICATOR

There are 8 fundamental traits of an effective communicator. Effective communication skills may seem elusive and unattainable, but truthfully it's a matter of combining the 8 traits to create a magnetic personality. Be prepared to work through each trait – one per chapter – and embrace them as your own.

PART 3: YOUR CONNECTED LIFE

Great things come with time, effort, and practice. Part 3 is a practical and helpful guide through the various ways you can apply effective communication in everyday life. This is where you will learn to radiate a powerful presence and summon your best life with grit and determination. It holds the keys to great conversations, deep and profound relationships, and step-by-step walk-throughs of the basics through to the big stuff.

You can tackle these three parts at your own pace or you can follow the integrated 7-day format you'll find in your free, accompanying Workbook. Use the LearnWell Community along the way. The 7-day format is designed to challenge and motivate you  to learn effective communication in just one week. Its structure is well-balanced to maintain a level of capability and difficulty for a truly rewarding journey.

Be prepared to let go, feel something new, and open your heart to a new way of attracting your ideal life. And don't worry, it's not all that serious, there's plenty of room for fun along the way. Joy is at your fingertips. Turn the page now to Chapter 1 and meet me at the beginning of this journey to discover the profound impact effective communication can have. The timing is perfect. Let's get started.

PART 1

THE FOUNDATIONS OF EFFECTIVE COMMUNICATION

1

THE QUALITIES OF AN EFFECTIVE COMMUNICATOR

An Introduction To Effective Communication And Connection

"Deep human connection is the purpose and the result of a meaningful life and it will inspire the most amazing acts of love, generosity, and humanity."

– Melinda Gates

Connection isn't what you think. It's not the chemistry between a man flashing his Colgate smile and a woman who winks back across a crowded dancefloor. It isn't defined by outgoing, obnoxious, or narcissistic behavior. But it is an asset a person can have to live a phenomenal life. This book is going to show you how to create it.

Anyone can be an effective communicator. It's not a mystical gift that only some people have, and others do not. Effective communication is something you can learn, provided you have a deep desire to get everything you want out of life – in the right way.

I know you're here because that's what *you* want. There are things you've wanted for a long time but are somehow not getting. A job promotion, a romantic partner, a reputation for being the most interesting and enjoyable person in the room.

You want friends, you want money, and you want happiness.

Communicating effectively can help you get those things. But not in a way that puts others down and manipulates them. It can get you those things in a way you can be proud of and excited about. It makes you the person who naturally attracts the best in life. It makes you a magnet for success. If you don't think that's true, let me prove that it is.

THE IMPACT OF EFFECTIVE COMMUNICATION

There was a time in my life when I felt like the smallest, most insignificant person in the room. I suffered from pretty severe depression and anxiety, among other things. I saw myself as a defectively shy girl.

I was blind to why I didn't fit in and had no clue where to start my transformation. I wanted to be the girl whose friends couldn't wait to see her after summer break. I wanted nothing more than to be invited to parties and actually feel comfortable at one. I wanted to ditch the shy girl identity and be seen.

Throughout my teenage years and early twenties, I studied human behavior by observing people and social norms. I was determined to change things for myself. I got the help I needed, and my mental health improved significantly.

I didn't want to just fit in and be a part of the furniture anymore. I wanted the healing to continue until I reached my goal of thriving amongst people. I wanted to be the best possible version of myself. I wanted to leave people better off than when I found them. I wanted to spread good energy and create a life where that always came back to me.

But I couldn't do that by staying in my shell.

Over the years of putting knowledge into practice, the answer became very clear. I noticed that the people who stand out in life, magnetize success, and always get what they want in a positive way share one vital thing in common: They know how to communicate effectively!

To help paint a picture of what effective communication can do for you, I will start this book by describing one of the most magnetic people I know. A man who manages to light up rooms despite growing up with immense hardships. He is one of the many people who exhibit all 8 effective communication traits in this book and who inspired my transformation from a weak, unsure nobody to a confident go-getter who achieves everything she sets her mind to.

It's true. Noah has good looks on his side, with a slightly crooked smile, pale blue eyes, and dark, thick locks of hair. But looks have little to do with his presence.

The powerful leadership skills he possesses, paired with his gentle impressionability, are enough to make anyone feel secure around him. He has the ability to instill your unwavering trust in him, and he doesn't let you down. His sense of connection is in his presence and the way he makes people feel. A deep sense of connection to others is the result of knowing how to communicate.

Noah entered my life at a time when everything had fallen apart. I was unsure of myself, my value, and what I was capable of. I've always been a dreamer, but life got in the way of my self-esteem and confidence, which stopped me from going after what I wanted.

The humanity and care Noah showed when he met me made an impact that transformed me forever. He restored my faith in humanity and proved that the optimistic view of the world I like to have wasn't so far-fetched.

When I met Noah, I was in college. I was the new girl who had been invited to join his group of friends by a girl who saw me looking lost and upset. Noah stood relaxed against a balcony balustrade as everyone adjusted their position around him. With his right foot casually crossed over his left and his hands relaxed between subtle gestures, he delivered the punchline of his story. I couldn't help but join the laughter as his eyes shone with genuine enthusiasm. His story wasn't particularly special or uncommon, but his delivery lifted the energy of the group. The calm joy he embodied was infectious.

As the day went on, I became so comfortable and relaxed in this small group that I started to feel as though I was amongst friends. Whenever I would join in, some of them listened while others seemed distracted. But Noah's engagement evoked an outgoing side of me that I hadn't exercised in a while. I felt seen.

From that day, Noah and I became lifelong friends. But above all else, he emulated something that I wanted to become. Compared to my chaotic uphill world at the time, his seemed to flow so easily. He tackled problems like a salmon swimming upstream, knowing he would always come out on top.

In his professional life, Noah commands respect without needing to demand it. He is so secure in himself, despite every challenge he's been through, that he handles conflict with grace, honesty, and compassion. Sure, he loses his temper occasionally and can get frustrated when people mess him around, but he never uses his anger as an excuse to tear anyone else down.

He is always the first person in a crowd to welcome you and make you feel a part of something great. People never feel left out, insignificant, or bored in his presence. But the most unexpected trait of Noah's is that he's an introvert. His social battery can get drained easily, but he doesn't let that stop him from maintaining a full and enjoyable social life. He knows when to take time for himself and when he can give back.

As our friendship matured, I started to wonder how he did it. What makes him so magnetically warm and fun? What is the secret to his serene yet spirited nature? How did he become the confident, caring, charismatic man he is? I had similar questions about the other well-connected, magnetic people I had met up until this point.

I couldn't help but feel that they must all have been blessed at birth with such strength and valor to tackle life as if they had it all figured out. And what about the rest of us? Are we all innately doomed to be stressed out, awkward, and boring in social settings, relying on people like Noah to make us feel something again? I got my answers.

The truth is Noah is a highly effective communicator. That's what makes him so compelling. He's far from perfect. He gets angry, he makes mistakes. There have certainly been times when he's allowed stress to get the better of him, biting his nails as he pushes through a work deadline. He has lost his temper so badly that there is still a dent in the drywall of his mother's house from when he was a teenager. And I know he's had his fair share of arguments, even within the boundaries of his healthy relationships. But communicating effectively and connecting with people is not about being deceptively perfect or hiding your flaws. In fact, it is often the opposite.

You see, effective communication can have a profound effect on life's normalities. It can make the highs glisten with raw, authentic joy while it softens the landing of any falls and failures. You'll notice this pattern amongst all the stories throughout this book.

Well-connected people all seem to handle life with a unique sense of optimistic grit. That's the grit I want you to acquire.

Noah's profound level of communication skill is the oil that keeps the gears of his life turning smoothly. It helps him persuade people in a way that makes everyone feel like the winner. And it is built on such a strong sense of self-confidence and worth that he can quickly pick himself up and brush himself off when needed. He epitomizes the magic that true, effective communication can bear.

DEFINING EFFECTIVE COMMUNICATION

This is where I want to make something very clear: Effective communication is about being authentic. Once I got to know Noah and felt the integrity of his authenticity, I realized that being magnetic and influential was a skill only acquired through a profound desire to make life wonderful for yourself AND others.

It's less about convincing people to like you and more about being likable. It's an outward-focused perception of socializing. That means having extraordinary empathy for people. It's about your presence and how your aura draws people in and makes them feel something rare – acknowledged and accepted.

It's not about putting on a facade of bravado or shrinking yourself to fit in, but rather about being honest, open, and secure in yourself. It's about being able to lead completely and wholeheartedly with a sense of vulnerability that makes people follow you without question. Anyone can feel familiar with you because an effective communicator is not afraid of their flaws or failures. They're so confident in themselves that they see failure as lessons learned rather than something that diminishes their value.

Realizing that was the first step of my transformation. Then, I quickly began practicing and absorbing the traits I'm going to share with you in Part 2 of this book. I no longer had to force positive social interactions, work tirelessly for the career I wanted, or feel like I was wearing a mask just to make an impression on people. My charisma began to build until it became natural, quick, and effective. Then I learned how to communicate that magnetism, and everything changed.

I started to notice the ease in people around me. My laughter became infectious as my demeanor became light-hearted, confident, and fun. People, even strangers I would engage with in small talk, began to linger in conversation with me. Friends and family started heeding my advice and even seeking it. I landed the job of my dreams and very soon noticed the glistening joy that true, effective communication can bring to your life.

I felt of value to others, in both my personal and professional life, for the first time ever.

But let me clarify – this didn't happen because I suddenly became more objectively valuable, but rather because I wasn't afraid to embrace the value I already had and freely offer it to others.

Discovering my sense of authenticity and belonging formed an aura of attraction around me that seemed to magnetize the life I wanted. It didn't magically erase my struggles, but it seemed to form a bubble of optimism and security around me.

 The transformation that took place in my life after accepting that *I* have value and then learning how to communicate that value in my everyday life was so profound that I need to share what I've learned with you. However, before you move on to Chapter 2, find a moment to complete the exercise in your Workbook.

When you're done, I challenge you to turn the page and strap in for an exciting journey of transfiguration from average to exceptional. Rather than going years cluelessly trying to copy what you see from other happy and successful people – as I did – let me carefully reveal the code of connection to you so your life can change too.

WHY PEOPLE WHO COMMUNICATE EFFECTIVELY ALWAYS WIN

The Truth About Effective Communicators And Why Motive Matters

"Winning doesn't always mean being first. Winning means you're doing better than you've ever done before."

– Bonnie Blair

Lacing up my hockey shoes as the sun bore down on my shoulders, Anna stepped onto the astroturf. With a wide smile, she looked at me and asked, "Are you ready?" I swallowed nervously and nodded back, pushing myself up from the ground and adjusting my ponytail.

We were about to face off with the women's league hockey team. As the youngest members of our college's first team, Anna and I always stuck together. We'd both placed at tryouts and even though that meant we were good enough to be there, I was scared.

The women's team had the advantage of being stronger, older, and more experienced than ours. But there we were, about to fight for our place at the international hockey tournament of the year.

With the sound of hockey sticks colliding, girls shouting "Here!" in a bid for the ball, and the whistle of our referee interjecting, the game was lengthy and tough. By halftime, we were already exhausted, but the scores were close – women's league in the lead.

As we huddled together in our team circle, there was a growing consensus that if we kept pushing, we could still win. But with flustered cheeks and muscle fatigue, many of the girls were preparing themselves for a loss. Anna was next to me in the circle. As we broke the huddle with a competitive cry of "Hah!" she stopped me and looked me dead in the eyes.

"I'm going to make sure that whenever I get the ball, I pass it over to you. So make sure you stay open, okay?"

With an exhale of relief and a smile, I replied, "Okay." I was so glad that she had a plan and that she trusted me. Before this point, we had carried out our team strategy as usual, doing our part when we could as the two youngest players. But Anna knew I was fast and she wanted to win.

You see, Anna was part of the defense for our team, and I was what you call a "wing," that meant that it was up to me to get the ball to the goal strikers — the pressure was high. We played our hearts out for the rest of the game until the final whistle blew.

I wish I could tell you that we won by a long shot. I wish this story was as simple as "you can do anything you set your mind to, even if the odds are against you." But that wouldn't have much to do with this book, would it?

Don't worry, we didn't lose. The game ended in a tie, sending both teams to the international finals. But this chapter isn't about winning or losing. It's about why people who communicate effectively always win. That's where Anna comes in.

I believe that without Anna, we would've lost that game entirely. The extra goals we contributed played a big part in the outcome of the score. Her encouragement and trust in me made me feel like my efforts mattered, and I gave more energy to that second half of the game than any match I'd played before.

When the match was over, our team was overjoyed by the results. But with a rough game like that, many of the girls had some resentment towards the other team. Jessica's finger suffered a collision injury with another girl's stick. Stacy felt angered by the other team's competitiveness. And many of the other girls had worked so hard that their enthusiasm was depleted.

Now, Anna, she was different. She left that field with the same enthusiastic smile that she had walked onto it with. As we each shook the hands of the other players one by one, she gave each person a second of eye contact, a smile, and a "Thank you!" or a "Well done!"

When so many of the other girls could hardly muster a firm handshake, Anna genuinely appreciated the challenge that the women's league offered us. She showed each of the women acknowledgment, even if all she had was a second.

Walking off the field, Anna gave me a reassuring squeeze on the shoulder and quietly exclaimed, "We did it!" with a glow of her magical enthusiastic energy. We didn't win by score, but we did win by personal achievement.

That is how effective communicators always win. Let me elaborate.

BE A GOOD SPORT

If you want to become an effective communicator – which I know you do – you will have to adopt a new understanding of winning. Connected people, like Anna, don't see winning as a way to be better than others. They don't see other people's progress or success as competitive fuel. No, connected people view winning as a personal endeavor.

To move forward, I need you to answer a very simple question: "What is your motive behind wanting to communicate more effectively?" Go to your Workbook now and give it some thought before writing down your answer. Don't be shy or worried about whether your answer is noble. Just be honest with yourself. When you're done, come back and keep reading.

It's tough to find a balance between:

- Scenario 1: wanting to communicate more effectively to make friends, be influential, and leave a good impression out of personal gain.
- Scenario 2: wanting to communicate more effectively out of the deep desire to be the best person you can be to make a positive impact on the world.

Which scenario do you see as a win?

Whatever your answer is, I need you to know that choosing the first isn't necessarily bad. You can certainly want to make positive changes in your life through reading this book. But I want to encourage you to build a desire for the second scenario as well.

Why? Because the truth is, authentic connections, the kind that *really* makes your life amazing, come from being outward-focused. The most influential communication for positive change is the kind that benefits others - even if your motive is getting what *you* want out of life.

Yes, in my example, Anna used her positive trust and influence over me to encourage me in the hopes of winning the game. But she didn't see winning as beating the other team. She wanted to walk away from the match, proudly knowing that we did our best and gave the women's league a fair challenge. She wanted to give our team a chance at moving on to the international finals. She knew how hard each one of us had trained to be there, and she didn't want to be a part of the reason why our training went to waste.

More importantly, I want you to see her example as a truly effective way to **recognize** a win. Most people see getting first place as a win. But Anna appreciated the results of the match the same way she would have if we *had* come first. She reacted as if we did win fully and wholeheartedly.

A good sport takes any positive progress as a win. Effective communicators are good sports.

Most people struggle to identify wins in their everyday lives, but effective communicators see wins everywhere, and they know how to acknowledge them and celebrate them. What better way to attract more wins into your life than this?

Can you see how an honest "win" is nothing more than seeing personal progress? Sometimes, magnetizing more success in your life simply comes down to knowing how to recognize it.

THE INFLUENCE OF EFFECTIVE COMMUNICATION

Like Anna's bright smile helping to ease my anxiety before a match, effective communication gives you the unbelievable ability to make a positive impression on people. But there is a scientific explanation for why this happens. It's got to do with attractiveness. And I'm not talking about looks.

While looks can play a role, they aren't the most important thing when it comes to effective communication. Effective communication is most affected by perceived attractiveness rather than facial symmetry and appearance.

The more attractive someone perceives you to be, the more likely they are to view you in a positive light, trusting you more readily and leaning into what you say.[1] Your perceived attractiveness and charisma can also make you more influential.

A study[2] I find fascinating is one done on an experienced court jury where researchers tested the difference in reaction to two experts who presented themselves in very different ways.

The results showed that the jury was more likely to see an expert in the court as experienced, trustworthy, and reliable if they were charismatic and good at communicating in comparison to an expert of equal experience who presented themselves in a lifeless, boring way. The jury was even more likely to see this expert's evidence as more valuable to the case, even when the evidence wasn't substantial.

If an experienced jury can be undoubtedly influenced by effective communication, the skills you gain as you read this book will undoubtedly have an effect on the everyday people around you.

I'll get into how you can directly increase your perceived attractiveness in Chapter 10. But, for now, I need you to know that as you continue along this path, you'll already notice how people naturally treat you of higher value. That's a guarantee.

Communication and attractiveness work together to help people judge you in a more positive light. It is only instinctual for people to like you more when you can communicate with them more effectively. The key here being *with them*. This book is about nurturing your ability to change how people perceive you so you can magnetize the friends, relationships, and success you want.

You are already of value. It's only a matter of learning how to properly express and share that value with others. The more attractive and authentic you are *perceived* to be, the more trusted and influential you will be.

A POSITIVE OUTLOOK AND SOCIAL CONNECTION

As a sneak peek into building your perceived attractiveness, I need you to know that the magnetic appeal you feel when you are around people like Noah or Anna does not emanate from their physical appearance but rather from inside of them.

Communication includes the essence someone gives off. A noticeable positivity that makes you want to gravitate toward them. That's the easiest way to become more attractive instantly. Effective communicators have a positive outlook on life.

This reminds me of a quote from the poet Dorothy Parker, "Beauty is only skin deep, but ugly goes clean to the bone." The same applies to magnetism. If you are genuinely happy, confident, and positive inside, that energy shines through and automatically draws people in.

But let me take that one step further.

Not only do people like Anna have a positive outlook on life, but they find joy in other people's success. They are not only positive and happy in themselves, but they know how to be happy for others - in fact, it comes naturally.

You see, even a happy, confident, and positive person can still make people feel uncomfortable in their presence. Those traits do not sway people into liking you on their own. True magnetism takes those traits and projects them outward, helping reveal the good in everyone else, too.

That's why effective communication works so well in society. Humans are highly social creatures, which means that we need connections to survive. Effective communication helps to bridge the gap between who you are on the inside and other people.

Think about a lightbulb. The light source is the element inside the bulb. But what if the bulb was painted black? You wouldn't see how much light that bulb was emitting on the inside. Effective communication cleans away any barrier between your inner light and the outside world. Your light shines through authentically and fully in every moment.

Even if you're having a terrible day and your light source is low. You're still going to show so much more authenticity in comparison to someone who hides everything they feel.

But how do people go from a blacked-out bulb to openly sharing their authentic selves with others? Well, this varies from person to person.

ARE YOU BORN WITH IT?

While communicating effectively is not an innate skill, meaning that it is not something you are simply born with, your level of communication does have roots in your childhood. While effective communication is often passed down by parents, neglect in childhood can also cause someone to develop traits of effective communication.[3]

The positive childhood acquirement of effective communication is self-explanatory – we often learn how to behave from our parents' example. But when it comes to a negative childhood experience, like neglect, we can learn a lot more. This is where it's easy to see how anyone can learn how to become magnetic and connected.

If you think about a child or teenager in a neglectful household, they are lacking one of the most vital components to human health: social connection. One way to combat this problem is for them to analyze people in successful social interactions and apply what they learn to their own attempts to socialize. With the added desperation and need for connection, the effort put into being likable could easily build into a highly effective communication strategy.

We're looking at someone who has experienced struggle and knows how to empathize with others. They are almost hyper-aware of how other people feel around them. And they go the extra mile to make people feel happy and comfortable. They are also deeply fulfilled by positive social connections.

To drive this point home, let's compare the two people I have introduced you to so far: Noah and Anna. Anna is an extroverted woman who grew up in a privileged household with two loving parents and a lot of opportunities for academic and financial success. Noah is an introvert who grew up in poverty with his single mother working full-time to support them. Both grew up to be wonderfully effective communicators.

What we can see from this example is that so long as you have the drive to form authentic social connections and make an exceptional impact on people, you can learn to be magnetic. It doesn't matter what kind of childhood you had, or what personality traits you feel you do or don't have. Your ability to connect is going to be a unique essence of magnetism that only you can provide. So if you're ready to learn effective communication, turn the page now and get excited. Your personal journey to connection has begun.

3

HOW YOU CAN COMMUNICATE EFFECTIVELY

Unlocking Your Potential To Connect And Find Success

"Communication is the sovent of all problems and is the foundation of personal development."

– Peter Shepherd

In Part 2 of this book you're going to learn the fundamental traits that you need to build an effective communication strategy. But before we move on, there is a very confronting question I need to ask you: Are you willing to face the parts of yourself that are boring, unattractive, and ugly?

It might sound harsh, but to truly transform into someone who is interesting, magnetic, and able to connect with others you need to start from a humble place. And, you need to be willing to transform the parts of yourself that don't align with effective communication.

Think about it like this. If I put an unopened chocolate bar on the table in front of you and spent some time hyping you up about eating it, how would you feel? You might imagine taking a bite and feeling the sweet notes of chocolate and caramel hit your tongue.

Now what if I unwrapped the bar only to reveal an inedible piece of plastic? You might feel disappointed, angry, and duped.

That is exactly what will happen if you don't move forward with the genuine intention of becoming a better version of yourself. If your intentions are to simply create a persona that you can use to trick people into liking you, this book won't help.

I'm not here to give you surface-level tips and tricks. I deeply and passionately want you to confidently attract and build real, authentic connections with people. I want the core of who you are to shine through and become so attractive that people can't help but gravitate towards you. I want you to build genuine, long-lasting magnetism – to the core of your person.

If you're still with me, I know that you're here for the right reasons. I'm also certain that you already have a lot of fantastic traits that make you likable. I'm not about to give you a list of traits that will erase who you really are. It's only a matter of fine-tuning your ability to openly and honestly share who you are with others.

These next 8 chapters are very practical and real, giving you the tools you need to break free from the things holding you back. But it's going to require that you change gears and prepare to put in effort.

EMBRACING YOUR POTENTIAL

There is a finesse to effective communication, and part of that means going through a transfiguration. You have to let go of the parts of yourself which don't serve you or others, and embrace new traits you might not have thought were available to you.

You see, someone who was once shy, insecure, and defensive could transform into a person who is socially comfortable, confident, and at ease with themselves. Any traits that hold you back from the life you want are erasable. You can shift them with time and conscious effort. I know this because I've done that.

It's the same way someone who is self-centered, negative, and closed off can grow their empathy, shift their outlook on life, and open themselves to new connections. Embracing a deep and authentic shift like this in your personality is the only way you're going to move forward. Let me show you how to do that.

These next 8 chapters will give you the tools to become the rich, delicious chocolate you say you are and not a plastic replica. They're going to show you how to discover your ability to connect, fully accept it as a part of who you are, and then watch it naturally attract people like a moth to a flame.

Every effective communicator has certain traits in common that when combined create a force of allure and charisma that seems to simply emanate from them. However, you should know that none of the traits in Part 2 are innate. They are all things you can learn and master, no matter who you are or how far off you feel from being a great communicator.

Once you apply these traits and allow them to gradually build into unshakable confidence, you won't need to do much else. You'll notice yourself naturally lighting up the room you walk into, finding the right things to say at the right times to truly enchant people, and building the deep and lasting connections you've needed for a lifetime. Then, once you're there, Part 3 will take you all the way. Don't stop now. Keep going.

All I ask of you right now is to be open to absorbing the information I'm about to share with you. I know that if you let it sink in without resistance, it will change you. You have a well of untapped potential within you, waiting for you to let it flow.

Knowing and trusting that effective communication skills are enough to unlock a completely new life for yourself, keep reading with new eyes and an absorbent mind. This is the only way new information can influence your life without any barriers affecting your understanding.

You also need to embrace your potential and be willing to do the work it takes to meet your own expectations. All the information you need is in this book, but only you can put the information to practice. Trust that it'll be worth it and take action.

In a world where social media has been placed on a pedestal, making small talk is seen as an inconvenience, and deep, authentic social connections feel rare. Effective communication can take you anywhere.

It's the elixir of life that keeps you connected, understood, and open to new experiences. And it all comes down to simple traits and skills that you can practice to improve life for yourself and everyone in it.

I want to show you how a deeper sense of connection to the world and the people around you will turn your life around forever. From financial success to everyday fulfillment, let me guide you through this monumental shift. From boring to exciting, repelling to attractive, darkness to light – connection is yours if you want it.

 As you explore the following traits, you'll notice they build like bricks to a solid foundation of effective communication. Take a moment now to reflect on Part 1 in your Workbook, then turn the page and let me reveal the first secret of this skill that you can start applying right now.

Note: If you are following the 7-day Workbook challenge, then this will be the end of Day 1. Good on you! Come back tomorrow and turn the page to start Day 2 of your effective communication journey.

In a world where social media has been placed on a pedestal, making small talk is seen as an inconvenience, and deep, authentic social connections feel rare. Effective communication can take you anywhere.

PART 2

TRAITS OF AN EFFECTIVE COMMUNICATOR

START WITH YOU

Developing Self-Awareness For A Complete Transformation

"Self-awareness is the ability to take an honest look at your life without any attachment to it being right or wrong, good or bad."

– Debbie Ford

TRAIT 1: SELF-AWARENESS

Earphones firmly plugged into my ears, I drowned out the sound of the boys behind me on the bus. They had been making hurtful jokes about me, followed by obnoxious laughter. Not wanting to let them win, I restrained my tears.

However, the bullying continued almost daily, and many of my friends began joining in as well. I don't blame myself for developing low self-esteem when I was experiencing this kind of bullying at the young age of 14.

Soon I was defeated, feeling very lonely, and convinced that people suck. I started going to school and trying to make new friends. While it worked to some degree, I still sat with different groups of my peers each lunch break. I didn't really fit in or belong anywhere.

However, it's not like me to give up easily, and I decided something had to change. This is where my analytical observancy came in handy. Over the summer, I went into "research mode." I wanted to know how to become more popular with the girls in my grade.

At the time, the internet wasn't the incredible resource it is today, with YouTube videos, podcasts, and easy access to research papers. So, as silly as it sounds, I relied on movies. You name it, any teenage high school movie you could think of, I watched it, keenly observing the social dynamics between the popular kids.

I'm not about to tell you that it worked wonders. I'd also never suggest anyone mistake cinema for real life. It did work for a while, but it was not the solution I thought it was.

Yes, I managed to fake my way into being invited to every party, sleepover, and lunch break with the popular girls. But when I suddenly had to leave the school, none of them bothered to contact me. I wasn't invited to a single party over the holidays, a single sleepover, or even a group chat. It was as if the friendships I built never existed at all.

The truth is, they didn't. Not really.

Like the chocolate bar analogy from Chapter 3, I was parading myself around as a confident people-loving, partygoer when, in reality, I was still depressed, insecure, and secretly bitter. It was false advertising – a plastic chocolate in a shiny wrapper.

None of the friends I made with my superficial efforts lasted. I could never crack the surface and find a real human connection with them. We barely spoke about anything real, personal, or of genuine interest to me. But when they didn't reach out to support me, I still painted them as bad friends and lived with a victim mentality for many years.

You see, I lacked the first fundamental trait of effective communication, something that opens you up to the truth behind every failed social interaction you've ever had. It's what makes you realize where *you* went wrong and eventually leads to understanding others better. It's the only way forward if you want to improve yourself for good. It starts with you. It's self-awareness.

Only later in life did I realize something. If I wasn't genuinely enjoying my friendships, how could I expect others to? If I was only offering my support out of personal gain, how could I build deep connections with people? If I was giving off a gloomy and depressed demeanor, it's no wonder so many of my peers stopped wanting to be around me — at least, it played a role in that. I was going about this process completely wrong — fully concerned with whether people liked me rather than if I was someone worth liking.

Of course, there was a sense of naivety about my perception before, but the lesson I learned is still valuable to me now. I learned that your life will reflect whatever you have inside yourself. Unless you build self-awareness and start working on your inner light, you will not send the message you want to send to people.

Maybe on first impression, you might seem like someone exciting and interesting, but with time — and it doesn't take long — people will always come around to the truth about you.

Remember what I said in Chapter 1: Effective communication is less about convincing people to like you and more about being likable.

So, I urge you to use this chapter to start your journey toward communicating effectively from the inside out. Rather than wasting time trying to skip ahead and flip through these traits, I want you to really pay attention here. Your journey MUST start from within, or else you risk never seeing the results you came here to find.

WHO ARE YOU?

Let's start by taking a moment to think about what you're working with. Who are you? Or rather, what kind of person do you see yourself as? Answer this question in your Workbook and then complete the rest of the exercise waiting for you there. This exercise is designed to help you find a starting point for you to refer back to later on. There's nothing better than having a "proof of progress" to look back on.

Now that you have a solid reference point for how you see yourself get ready for that perception to shift rapidly. I know you might be certain that you know yourself best, but the truth is, other people, even strangers, may have an advantage over you.

Just think about it. How many times have you encountered someone who makes an impact on you, but if you point out their strengths, they react with denial? Or, on the flip side, you meet someone who is unfriendly and blunt, only to confront them and notice their utter confusion at your reaction.

You see, often, your perception of yourself might not be translating the way you think it is. Maybe you're having a great morning, and someone asks why you look down. Perhaps you feel like you need a friend, but nobody seems to notice the subtle shift in your mood. Or, you might wonder why, no matter how hard you try, people don't seem to take you seriously.

Like 95%[4] of the population, you probably think you have self-awareness when in fact, you don't. Now, I'm not saying that there isn't a possibility that you do it, but I'm going to invite you to do an exercise that might change your mind. Either way, you will gain valuable insights.

Start asking people in your life how they perceive you. To make it simple and get honest answers, ask them what they think your greatest strength is and what they think your greatest weakness is. There are a few pages in your Workbook for you to take note of the answers you get. Chances are, different people will give you different answers, and you'll end up with a list of strengths and weaknesses you might not have ever associated with yourself before. Plus, if multiple people give you the same answer, pay attention – whether you agree with them or not.

You can take your time with this and continue reading as you build up your idea of who other people think you are. While this exercise might upset you as parts of your self-image are potentially shattered, I want you to consider the bigger picture.

Other people's perspectives are not necessarily a reflection of who you *really* are but rather how you are perceived – which reveals your communication flaws.

Maybe you've got great traits that go unnoticed because you lack confidence. Or perhaps you're a great communicator on the surface, but you struggle to take conversations deeper. Whatever comes from this exercise, above all, it will help nurture your self-awareness.

You see, self-awareness comes from taking a moment to ask questions about yourself. You need to get curious about who you are and how you can grow. It's not about analyzing your traits and accepting them. It's about taking what you learn and making the changes necessary to be who you want to be – the best version of yourself.

Once you have asked at least 5 people about your strengths and weaknesses, take a moment to compare the two lists: yours and theirs. Are there any traits that coincide? Are there traits you agree with but didn't think about before? Maybe there are some you don't agree with at all. Just take it all in.

Looking at the list of strengths you now have, go to your Workbook and start a list of strengths you would like associated with you. Use the lists you've already made, but think about whether there are any strengths you would like to acquire.

If you don't know yet, you can use the traits of effective communication as inspiration. Give it some thought and start adding to the list, thinking about what strengths the best version of yourself has. Take time to reflect on this list as we continue. Come back to it and add more if you like.

FROM PAPER TO PRESENCE

Self-awareness is not something that will form overnight. It is a habit that you need to nurture along your journey. You don't need to constantly question everything you do or beat yourself up for mistakes. In fact, doing those things can significantly harm your self-awareness. But what you must focus on is how you come across to others. I'm talking about your aura, your energy.

No, I don't mean the colorful rays of energy that psychics will tell you they see around you. I'm talking about your presence. You must be aware of how you present yourself and how that translates to others.

Remember this: Energy is honest.

Energy is honest.

SPEAK EASY

You can't hide who you are because people can feel your energy before you've even spoken a word. It speaks volumes on your behalf. It's also going to affect your perceived attractiveness greatly. That's why you need to transform from the inside out.

As we move forward, I want you to think about bringing the positive traits you've written down to life. I want you to take what I'm about to teach you and use it to transfer your ideal self from paper to presence.

Even if your self-awareness feels strange, confronting, and maybe insignificant, trust that it will grow into something bigger. Eventually, the more you can tune into yourself, your negative patterns, and unwanted traits, the quicker you will unlock the seductively positive traits you're here for.

But whatever you do, don't skimp on this. Make an effort to really get to know yourself and understand where your positive traits are lost in translation. Don't worry about having it all figured out right now. As you continue, you will find that more truths about yourself start to surface. However, until you reach the final page of this book, keep growing your self-awareness.

Reflect. Become aware. Stay open to change.

Finally, you must understand that none of these 8 traits are overnight accomplishments. You have to trust the process and stick around for the results. Give it your all, and don't take them for granted. Each trait fits together seamlessly to usher in the life you want. So, while your self-awareness is budding, let's continue the chain and move on to the next vital link – empathy.

Note: Self-awareness is one of the most important traits of effective communication, the one that will allow you to succeed in all others. This is the end of Day 2 of your 7-day journey. Allow what you've learned to sink in before returning tomorrow for Day 3.

5

WITHOUT THIS, YOU ARE IRRELEVANT

The Power Of Empathy And How To Build It

"Empathy is the engine that powers all the best in us. It is what civilizes us. It is what connects us."

– Meryl Streep

TRAIT 2: EMPATHY

"It's a cutthroat industry." "We live in a dog-eat-dog world." "My hands are tied."

These are the kinds of things we hear all the time in business. While you claw and climb for your taste of success, phrases like these will likely come along to put doubt in your mind. They're the kinds of phrases that lead you to believe emotions have no place in business.

Truthfully, phrases like these have no place in business. They lack the most important thing for success in any industry or area of your life – empathy.

Now, listen carefully.

The difference that empathy can make in leadership roles is insurmountable. It can mean the difference between happy, hardworking employees and uninspired employees constantly on the lookout for better opportunities.

But why does this have anything to do with effective communication? Because people who can communicate effectively are leaders. They exude a sense of confidence and comfort that makes people willing to follow them and trust their advice. If you want to become a leader, win people over, and find success in life, you need to manifest a powerful sense of empathy. You need to apply this lesson to everything you do.

Every moment you are around other people is an opportunity to lead.

How you take that statement comes down to how you see leadership. Do you see it as a way to get what you want by controlling a group of people? Or do you see it as a skill that can harness their passion and willingness to work towards a mutually beneficial outcome?

The truth is, maybe the first approach will work out in the short term, but if you want high-value employees who will fully commit to your ideas and feel inspired to work hard for you, the latter is the only approach worth taking.

You see, successful leadership isn't a way to sit on a throne of power, take control, and come out on top. It's a powerful role that should only be used with the best intentions. Becoming a great leader is how you can keep your unfading reputation of strength and admiration forever. And it starts with empathy.

WHAT IS EMPATHY AND HOW TO GET IT

Empathy is your ability to recognize how someone else is feeling and knowing how to act accordingly. Your level of empathy lies in how well you can put yourself in the shoes of another. It's your care for the way they feel, followed by your caution to help improve the situation.

Let me repeat that: Empathy is your care, followed by your caution. It's not only in your ability to recognize someone's feelings but also in how you behave afterward.

As an example, if you notice a young child who lost their balloon at an amusement park, an empathetic approach would include 3 aspects.

1. You would *understand* that the child feels sad having lost their balloon.
2. As an adult, you might realize that a lost balloon is a silly thing to cry about but with empathy, you would be able to *differentiate* your feelings from the child and understand why they might be sad about losing a balloon even when you would not.
3. If you had to engage with the child, you would take caution for their feelings and *show* them understanding and comfort.

Again, you would understand the situation, be able to differentiate your feelings from theirs, and show your empathy in a comforting way.

Of course, it is easy to dismiss someone else's feelings based on how you might feel in the same situation. But empathy allows you to look past that barrier and know that no matter how small a problem seems to you, it could be a big problem to someone else, and that is perfectly valid.

Another way to look at it would be to accept that if you were truly in another person's shoes, you would likely be reacting the exact same way. Never assume that you would do things differently had you been born into someone else's life.

Remember, if you think someone is overreacting, it's probably just because you're ignorant. There's likely more to the story than what you see. Knowing and trusting this fact is empathy.

Now I want to challenge you to see where else empathy can play a positive role in your life. We've already covered business, so think about your friendships, romantic relationships, and general interactions with people. Any situation involving two people can benefit from a dash of empathy.

Let's think about the way you treat servers at a restaurant. It takes empathy to care about the way you speak to them. If you put yourself in a waiter's shoes, it's easier to understand their mistakes and go easy on them when they happen.

Now try it on conflict. When you're upset with someone, take a moment to imagine what it's like to be them and try to understand more about their behavior. You might realize that their actions feel justified, and you're able to release your anger toward them more easily. Empathy reminds you that there is often much more going on in a person's mind that contributes to the magnitude of emotions and, therefore, reactions.

Next, why not use it to feel happier for people?

If your friend just got a promotion, your sister got engaged, or a child is experiencing something great for the first time, take a moment to put yourself in their shoes and feel the joy move through you. Showing empathy in a positive moment can not only help you respond appropriately, but you also get to share in someone else's joy. Isn't that wonderful?

Speaking of responding appropriately, as we've already established, there's more to empathy than simply putting yourself in someone else's shoes. That's just the beginning. The next and possibly the most important stage of having empathy is adjusting your behavior.

Empathy shouldn't be an internalized experience. True empathy should be felt by the people around you. Remember, there are three aspects to empathy. It's not just about feeling and understanding. It's about showing.

Your sense of empathy for people should affect your energy and give you better responses, especially during conflict. Remember what we said in Chapter 2, authentic connections come from being outward-focused. And people who communicate effectively care about making a positive impact on other people. That takes empathy.

If you can actively adjust your behavior in response to the unique interaction you're having with someone, you will offer a more helpful presence at that moment.

For example, if you meet someone and you pick up that they feel down, you can soften your approach, lower your voice, and offer more comforting words. Or, if you talk to someone who is cheerful about something, you can lift your smile, increase your energy, and add to the joy of the moment. If you're in conflict with someone, empathy gives you the opportunity to understand their perspective and diffuse the situation.

Through and through, empathy allows you to bring a benefit to any situation you find yourself in. I want you to adopt all the traits of someone who can communicate effectively but let empathy remain a priority as we continue.

I want you to be the person who makes people feel seen in a group of strangers. I want you to be the person people trust with their vulnerability. I also want you to share in the joyful pulse of a vibrant crowd, adding your unique magnetism to every interaction. But none of that is possible without genuine empathy. So, let me show you how to build it in 5 simple steps.

THE 5 STEPS TO BUILDING EMPATHY

Again, regardless of the level of empathy you have right now, it's not going to grow overnight – at least not significantly. The kind of authentic empathy I want you to build takes practice, conscientiousness, and a genuine desire to do right by others.

I know you care about people to some degree. Maybe you care about them a lot! Either way now is your chance to build on that and make the impact you want to make.

Step 1: Become Present Around People

It doesn't help being stuck in your head when you're around people. If you're too consumed in your own thoughts, anxieties, and to-do lists, you won't be open to connection. I need you to make a conscious effort to bring yourself out of your head and into the present moment instead.

You can ground yourself in the present with mindfulness techniques like grounding. This is when you take a moment to focus on each of your senses. Tuning into your senses will bring you into the present moment. Go to your Workbook and try it out right now!

If you struggle with anxiety around people, I urge you to start addressing and working through it. Grounding yourself will help. Any kind of mindfulness practice will improve your anxiety and make this journey so much more rewarding.

Step 2: Put Yourself Aside For A Moment

Even the best people become caught up in their own lives and problems. However, empathy is not about you. Get out of the habit of self-absorption and put yourself aside for a moment. When you are around people hoping to make a fantastic impression and form new connections, you must put whatever is on your mind aside and be open to listening to others.

Don't go into any conversations thinking about what *you* can gain from *them*. Switch it around entirely. I need you to put your focus on showing up as your best self in an attempt to improve *their* interaction with *you*.

Step 3: Get Curious About Them

Once you are ready to fully engage with someone, get curious about them. Allow your mind to wonder about who they are, what they're going to say next, and how they're feeling. Now that you're in the present moment and you've put yourself aside make sure you are completely focused and interested.

Just think about it: if you couldn't care less about the person you're talking to, they're going to pick up on that. This will likely cause them to close up, stop sharing, and lose interest in you. Remember, a huge part of empathy is genuinely caring about people.

Step 4: Listen To Understand, Not Respond

As you start to notice people light up in conversation with you as they realize they've found someone who is genuinely interested in what they have to say, listen. It's as simple as that.

But don't just take in the words they're saying while you load up on responses. Listen with the intention of understanding them. Don't listen to respond, listen to understand – more on this in Chapter 8.

It's too easy to focus on what you're going to say next. But a conversation is not two people fighting for the spotlight. The best connections are formed during conversations that flow naturally in a balanced way, creating a nice give-and-take.

The next and final step is a great conversation lubricant. But unless you can listen well and gain an understanding of the person you're speaking with, step 5 will lead to nothing. So *listen*.

Step 5: Make Your Questions Count

Questions are a surefire opportunity to ooze empathy in conversation. But you have to approach them in the right way. Rather than blurting out the same boring questions you'd expect in small talk, or asking uninspiring yes/no questions, I want you to dig a little deeper. Ask questions that are relevant, encouraging, and open-ended.

For example, if someone is telling you a story about their passion for running you could ask a question like, "Tell me about the first time you realized you love to run?" or "If I wanted to get into running, what advice did you wish you got at the start?" These questions leave plenty of room for the person to elaborate, showing that you have been paying attention and that you care about their opinions, stories, and feelings.

To ask these kinds of compelling questions, you need to master steps 1-4. The more in tune you are with the person, the more on-point and substantial your questions can be. Again, keep this in mind until you get to Chapter 8.

Of course, there's more to truly advancing your empathy and transporting people with your energy. But that lies in the topic of the next chapter. Remember, empathy isn't only about understanding and caring about people. It's also about how you make people feel, in other words, how you *show* them empathy. That's where this next link to the chain of effective communication comes in – nonverbal communication.

Without this special communication skill, your energy is weak, your light bulb is dim, and your chocolate wrapper is misleading. Turn the page to Chapter 6, and let's get started. This is where you *really* become intriguing.

6

THE REASON FOR 90% OF YOUR SUCCESS IN COMMUNICATION

The Words People Use Matter Far Less Than Everything Else

"The most important thing in communication is to hear what isn't being said."

– Peter Drucker

TRAIT 3: PRESENCE

Conflict and confrontation used to spiral me out of control. I'd feel overwhelmed instantly and struggle to keep my reactions in check. I'd become a mess. My heart would race and my body would tremble regardless of how hard I fought to compose myself. But one day I had an "Aha!" moment – a moment where something just clicked.

I finally understood the role that my presence played – something I soon discovered was simply a matter of exceptional non-verbal communication.

Almost every day, like clockwork, my partner and I would argue. He'd say something that would trigger an emotional response in me, and before I knew it, we'd be arguing for hours.

Over and over again, the arguments continued. Sometimes they were about small things, and sometimes bigger things. But the pattern was always the same. He'd confront me about something, I'd react emotionally and respond in a whiny tone of voice, and the situation would escalate. We'd made a habit out of it.

But one day, after hearing him point out my distressing tone of voice for the millionth time, I did something differently. Albeit a sarcastic response, it worked! I suddenly adjusted my tone and began replying in a calm, smooth voice. "There, is this better?" I said mockingly. To my surprise, he let out a massive, genuine sigh of relief and said, "Thank you." before sitting down calmly.

Confrontation was my trigger, but my tone was his. It was simply a miscommunication of non-verbal cues.

What I learned is that I can strongly influence how people receive my message by being aware of my presence – my energy – and adjusting my non-verbal communication accordingly.

Let me repeat that: You can influence how people interpret your presence by adjusting your non-verbal communication.

I know it's not always easy to reply and react in a loving, kind, or thoughtful way, especially not while you're angry, overwhelmed, or anxious. Emotions play a huge role in your non-verbal communication. But it's important that you understand that your presence at any given moment will influence how others respond to you more than the words you use. And there are many non-verbal cues that will impact your presence.

Things like your tone of voice, body language, gestures, and facial expressions, among others. Each nonverbal communication cue tells a story of its own and can dramatically influence how our message is received.

In fact, according to Albert Mehrabian, Ph.D., nonverbal communication, including tone, constitutes 93% of all in-person communication. That leaves just 7% for your words to play a part.

Dr. Merhabian's studies were about the magnitude of non-verbal communication during a conversation. Although each person expresses themselves non-verbally in a unique way, there are greater patterns within non-verbal communication that we can address within ourselves and adjust to shift our presence into a more accurate display of our intentions.

You can influence how people interpret your presence by adjusting your non-verbal communication.

Just as I learned to adjust my tone of voice during an argument, even though my instinct was to become whiny or yell, we can adjust most of our nonverbal cues to better communicate what we *mean* to say.

You already know that your *energy* determines your presence. Now I want to be clear that your energy is greatly determined by your non-verbal communication, even above your actions and words.

SHIFT YOUR ENERGY

I know the topic of 'energy' can be a bit obscure. I mean, what *is* energy? How do you define something you can't see, hear, or touch? You know you feel it when you're around people, but why? Are you picking up on some unseen force, or is there a more logical explanation? And best of all, can you hack it? Can you *choose* what energy you give off?

The simple answer is yes. To all of it. Your energy is a complex force of information you are sending at any given moment. But it isn't a force of mysterious wavelengths or "vibes." Your energy lies in the subtle, often subconscious, non-verbal communication cues that are happening every millisecond. This is often what people are 'hearing', regardless of what you're actually saying. They are picking up on your non-verbal communication cues and making an interpretation about who you are.

This brings us back to Chapter 4 – energy is honest. Your presence reveals your true nature and intentions even when you're trying your best to conceal them with words.

Think about the last time you asked a friend how they were doing, and they replied with, "I'm fine," even though you could practically smell it on them that they weren't okay. This is a perfect example of their presence – their energy – communicating something different from what they were saying.

Now let me ask you this: Which one did you trust? Did you trust their words, or did you read between the lines and listen to their non-verbal cues screaming the truth at you?

Every time you enter a conversation, your presence is doing the same. It's leaving you an open book with pages full of "I don't want to be here," "This person is so boring," and "Maybe if I smile and nod, she won't know I don't care." If your inner light is dim, your nonverbal communication cues will be your tell.

That's why if you want to shift your energy to convey "Hey! Come talk to me!" through the adjustment of your non-verbal communication cues. But you have to let the shift run deep. Starting from the most basic communication cues like body language or tone of voice and progressing to sending the right subconscious nonverbal cues like microexpressions.

MASTERING THE 8 VITAL NON-VERBAL CUES

The following forms of communication are all tools you have at your disposal to influence how your messages are being received. However, that's only one side of the story. As you know, there's always another party to the conversation. As you master these communication cues, you'll understand more about what others are truly communicating and your interpretation skills will become sharper.

Step 1: Posture & Proxemics

The first and easiest nonverbal cue you can adjust is your posture and proxemics. This is the way you take up space with your body and how close you stand to other people. For example, if you tend to make yourself smaller with your body posture – hunched over and arms crossed – and you like to keep your distance from people, you will likely come across as unapproachable and uncomfortable.

But before you can change your posture and proxemics, you need to understand a few things. Firstly, different cultures consider different proxemics appropriate or inappropriate. For example, some cultures might consider standing close to someone as friendly, while others might consider it aggressive. Of course, this will also depend on circumstances. But for the purpose of this book, I'm going to stick with Western culture, trusting that you will adjust what you learn to fit your culture.

Starting with proxemics, the easiest thing to adjust, there are different meanings for different distances kept between two people. In general, there are four "zones" of proxemics, also known as personal space. They include:

- Intimate: 0-2 ft
- Personal: 2-4 ft
- Social: 4-12 ft

- Public: 12 ft or more

These are the distances considered appropriate in different settings. They will vary from person to person, but in general, bide by these personal space rules to keep people feeling comfortable and respected around you.

Next, when it comes to body posture, keep it simple. Observe closed posture, neutral posture, and understand what open postures may be conveying. They can look like this:

Closed posture:

- Tightly crossed or folded arms
- Holding something against your chest or stomach
- Legs rigidly crossed over
- Legs slanted away from the conversation
- Tensely positioned feet
- Hunched shoulders
- Head hanging lower

Neutral posture:

- Sitting or standing up straight
- Head in a neutral position
- Hands rested on lap or table
- Shoulders relaxed but square

Open posture:

- Standing up straight
- Shoulders back
- Arms relaxed at sides
- Chin slightly upward
- Sitting with a slight lean forward
- Standing with feet apart

I need you to know that this is very general. Nonverbal communication is complex. Many of the other factors you're going to learn about will affect your posture as well as the situation, the topic of conversation, your relationship with the person you're talking to, your culture, and your gender.

For example, sitting with your knees apart can signal confidence in men but could be deemed inappropriate or off-putting in women. Or, standing up straight with your hands confidently perched on your hips can be great in a business presentation, but if you're at a funeral, it's a different story.

Another thing you should know before we move on is that closed body posture isn't always bad, and it doesn't mean you are an unfriendly person. In fact, crossed arms isn't the negative habit many people think it is, it's actually your natural self-soothing response. You are essentially giving yourself a hug and subconsciously protecting yourself. It simply reveals your discomfort.

However, if you want to intentionally send a better message to those around you, I suggest making an effort to at least soften your crossed arms. There's a very big energy shift between tense, tightly held arms that pull your body into a smaller position and soft, relaxed arms that signal comfort even though they're crossed.

Lastly, before we continue, remember that less is more with open posture. Even though having an open posture is the best way to give off an approachable, confident energy in seconds, you shouldn't be trying to max out your openness.

Too much of a good thing can be bad. If you try too hard here, you might come across as arrogant or smug with a superiority complex. People who communicate effectively usually have the perfect mix of a relaxed and confident open body posture.

Step 2: Facial Expressions

More difficult to control than your posture and proxemics, facial expressions are the most instant, surface level nonverbal communication. It's the easiest and quickest way to interpret how someone is feeling or what they're thinking.

Just think about the wide range of emotions a face can express. From elated joy to shock and despair, your face can tell it all. Adjusting your facial expressions isn't about trying to force a fake smile or feign surprise at a boring story. It's about making sure your face accurately conveys the message you're trying to.

You might be sending the wrong message with your facial expressions without even realizing it. It's also common to overdo them and overwhelm people in conversation with exaggerated expressions. I know because I tend to be on the more expressive side!

The solution here is to pay attention to how people respond to you and work to resolve any problems you may have. For example, if people often wonder why you hardly react when they tell you an exciting story, you may want to work on how your face expresses your surprise or interest. On the other hand, if people make big eyes at your over-exaggerated expressions or give you the impression that you're "too much," you may want to make sure you aren't overdoing it.

The best way to adjust and work on your facial expressions is in the mirror. You'd be surprised how most of the best public speakers, comedians, and leaders practice their words and expressions this way. It'd be a shame to let this highly effective self-improvement tool go to waste out of fear of looking silly. So, make use of your mirror!

This exercise will be in your Workbook to refer back to easily. But all you have to do is practice your facial expressions in the mirror. Use your imagination to rehearse conversations with people and try out different ways to respond with your face. You can also repeat conversations you've already had in your head and respond the way you remember responding only this time you get to see what you might have looked like. Take what you see, take it as a learning curb, and adjust it until you feel it's improved.

Step 3: Eyes, Eyes, Eyes

There is a natural eye-contact dance that should happen in a comfortable, enjoyable conversation. Too intense, and you're hogging the dance floor, too weak and you're left behind. Make sure that your eye contact is equal and complimentary to the amount of eye contact the other person makes.

For example, if you're speaking to someone more shy, soften your eye contact so as to avoid furthering their discomfort. However, if you're talking to someone about a serious topic that requires your full attention, you should make more meaningful eye contact that shows you're fully invested in the conversation.

Remember, your eyes lead the way. If you avoid eye contact and keep looking around the room, the person you're talking to might mistake you as uninterested or distracted.

Use your empathy and self-awareness to adjust your eye contact to the situation, person, and topic of discussion. If you find your increased eye contact causes the person to look away more, ease up. If they make more eye contact with you as they lean in and tell you something more serious, try to match their intrigue and attention.

Step 4: Paralanguage

Like my whiny tone aggravating every argument I had before adjusting it, I want you to acknowledge your paralanguage habits. Paralanguage refers to everything about the way you speak, excluding the words. For example, your tone, volume, pitch fluctuations, and filler sounds.

How you say something is twice as important as the words you use. For example, if you say, "Oh, don't be silly." in a condescending tone with a downward pitch fluctuation on the "don't," the statement will be offensive. But if you say, "Oh, don't be silly." in a light-hearted tone with an upward pitch on the "don't," it's much more likely to be considered a friendly statement. Throw in a giggle and a smile, and it's even better.

If you're unsure how to adjust your tone, practice saying things out loud in a different tone. To adjust your tone, think about the emotion you want to convey. If you want to convey anger, your tone will sound much more stern than if you want to convey kindness and love.

Try imagining the emotion you'd like to express while you say something out loud. Like practicing your facial expressions in the mirror, do the same with your tone, volume, and pitch fluctuations.

Another aspect of paralanguage you can practice to shift your energy from awkward and insecure to confident and magnetic is to ditch the filler sounds as much as possible. These are things like "ums" and "ahs." They are the sounds you make when you lose focus and hesitate in conversation. To speak more fluently and make a great impression, take enough time to think about what you want to say before opening your mouth. Get comfortable with a little silence, and speak when you are sure.

Step 5: Kinesics

More difficult to control than your body posture and proxemics, kinesics are a refined way to shift your energy in conversation using your body language. Kinesics are any movements and gestures you make involuntarily to communicate more efficiently.

Just to drive home how profound kinesics are in conversation, you should know that people who are born blind and people who are born with sight grow up to gesture the same in conversation as long as they're speaking the same language.[5] That's how intuitive and involuntary gestures can be.

The problem with kinesics is that they reveal much about how you truly feel. And if you feel uncomfortable or bored, your kinesics will clearly show that to the other person.

While microexpressions are similar, these facial expressions are so quick and short that they are hardly noticeable to yourself or the person you're speaking to. Only a subconscious message is received. But with kinesics, the automatic gesture is visible and often lasts longer than a microexpression. I'll speak on microexpressions in step 8.

Although you can only shift kinesics entirely through steps 7 and 8, they are much easier to control because you can visually see yourself making certain gestures or feel yourself making them. For example, an eye roll is a kinesic gesture. Or covering your face in shame. They are obvious and send a big message.

To shift your kinesics body language, I want you to start paying attention to your and other people's gestures in conversation. Grow an awareness for them. Notice when someone rolls their eyes and consider why. Notice how when you want to leave a conversation, you might quietly clap your hands together as you say, "Well, I better be going." Any body movements or gestures used to signal or communicate something are kinesics, and they can strongly impact the other person's interpretation.

Once familiar with your gesturing style, ask yourself how you might come across to others. Or better yet, if you were around someone who made the same gestures as you on a regular basis, how would you view them?

Step 6: Haptics

One of the most powerful and often overlooked forms of communication is touch, also known as haptics. Whether in a professional or romantic setting, how you interact with someone using touch matters.

An easy example of haptics is how you give and receive a handshake. If your hand is limp and lifeless, it could convey that you are inexperienced and unsure of yourself. If you are too rough, either squeezing too hard or shaking profusely, you might come across as domineering or arrogant. But if you reach out confidently and give a solid, even handshake, it is likely to be interpreted by the other person as assuredness.

Any time you use touch to communicate something, you need to be cautious. Always use empathy to gauge how the other person might interpret that touch. For example, in a social setting, if someone looks timid, don't approach them and give them a hard pat on the back. That could be alarming for them and make them wary of you. But, in the same social setting, if you see a friend of yours casually sitting and enjoying themselves, you could certainly go up and give *them* the same pat on the back as you greet them warmly. Making sure your presence is interpreted correctly means 'reading the room.'

Touch is one of the quickest and easiest ways to feel connected to someone. A simple touch can communicate various intentions without needing to say a word. Think about it, there are so many things a single touch can convey, such as:

- A gentle rub on the back during a hug: Warmth
- A soft squeeze on the shoulder: I see you
- A pat on the back: Good job!
- A soft whack on the shoulder after someone teases you: Playfulness
- Touching someone's hand during a sad story: Care
- Poking someone in the chest: Abusive dominance
- Pushing someone away from you: Self-defence
- Softly touching someone's face: Affection
- A rested hand on the lower back: Romantic connection

Isn't it amazing how describing a simple touch can paint an entire picture in your mind. You could feel each one of those, couldn't you? That's because touch conveys emotion in a physical way. You could close your eyes and block your ears and still feel the emotional intention of a single touch.

Before we move on to step 7, these are the 5 haptics categories you must know. I want you to keep them in mind as you continue to socialize and see if you can categorize any touches you see or experience. Try to understand haptics and apply what you learn.

A researcher by the name of R. Heslin, categorized haptics into 5 socially acceptable categories. They include:

- Functional: Expresses task orientation in a professional manner.
- Social: Expresses ritual interaction to convey politeness.
- Friendship: Expresses individual relationships in a warm manner.
- Love: Expresses emotional attachment and intimacy.
- Sexual: Expresses sexual intent.

Each category leaves room for both positive and negative touch. But, of course, positive touch will always get you much further than negative touch. Effective communicators never rely on any kind of forceful communication to get what they want. Their magnetism attracts it on its own.

Step 7: Physical Reactions

This is where things get interesting. This step and the final one delve into the realm of nonverbal communication that is out of your control. There is a host of cues you send out that are controlled by your subconscious mind and which can be interpreted in a way that is different from what you intend.

Physical reactions are your body's involuntary communication cues that reveal your true emotions to you or the people around you. They can include a racing heartbeat, sweating, blushing, or any other physical symptoms of emotion.

While you can't always control your physical reactions, this step requires a little less legwork to shift than step 8. Once you notice your body reacting to your emotional state, you can take steps to regulate your emotions and reduce the symptoms. It may take a few minutes to calm down or compose yourself, but it is definitely possible.

However, to prevent unwanted physical reactions, you will have to dig a little deeper. I want you to take time every day to regulate your emotions. There are many ways to do this, but some highly effective and popular techniques include deep breathing, mindfulness, positive self-talk, and therapy. You can work to reduce unwanted emotional reactivity that may trigger physical symptoms.

Unfortunately, once your emotions have reached the point of reactivity, it becomes noticeable and often offputting. Showing big emotions in a social setting is only human, but it can be distressing for people around you. Emotional regulation will help you choose when to process your emotions and when to keep them under control. The more in touch and comfortable you are with your emotions, the more relatable, vulnerable, and connected you will be.

Trying to conceal your emotions, such as intense nerves, anxiety, or anger, in a conversation is nearly impossible. No matter how hard you try, your emotions will reveal themselves in one way or another.

The ultimate management of how you are perceived comes from knowing how to alchemize your emotions, processing them in a healthy way, and becoming an emotionally stable person.

Emotional stability is a wildly attractive trait that not many people have mastered. Making an effort to know yourself and *feel* your way through difficult times will enhance your communication in a genuine and profound way.

Step 8: Microexpressions

Finally, the most difficult step in managing the messages you convey – your microexpressions. In the milliseconds between expressions, microexpressions reveal your subconscious thoughts and intentions.

There is nothing you can do to instantly fix microexpressions. If you secretly hate parties, it doesn't matter how much you smile, laugh, or crack jokes. Your disdain will show on your face. Maybe it won't show directly, meaning you likely won't see it in photos, and other people won't notice it directly, either. But microexpressions are our subconscious minds having a conversation with each other.

What I mean by that is your friends might not notice your microexpressions at all, but subconsciously, they will know something is up. These split-second reactions reveal your true intentions and nature, and there's nothing you can do to hide them. They are largely responsible for those times when you don't like someone but you can't really understand why. There's a good chance they aren't being genuine.

I don't want you to be one of those people. I want you to show up and be liked authentically and fully.

This nonverbal cue will influence your energy without you even knowing – it's the most honest of all. That's why you need to let your energy shift from deep within if you want to change your presence effectively. That means walking into a room and not having to feign joy, interest, or confidence. You must genuinely want to be the best version of yourself.

I know you've already been working on your strengths and weaknesses, but now I need you to work on something that will take every social interaction you have and guarantee your success. Once you fix this next big trait of effective communication, you won't have to fake anything anymore – your interest, engagement, and joy will be genuine without a doubt. It's the easiest way to attract an abundance of positive experiences in every aspect of your life. You need to adjust your attitude.

Note: Before you turn the page and work on your attitude, reflect on what you've learned throughout Day 3 and come back tomorrow to commence with Day 4. You're already almost halfway there!

7

HOW TO SHAPE YOUR ATTITUDE

The Power Of A Positive Attitude
And How To Adopt One

*"Your attitude, not your aptitude,
will determine your altitude."*

– Zig Ziglar

TRAIT 4: ATTITUDE

There is an incredible communication skill that I haven't revealed yet. It's so important, so powerful that it deserves a chapter of its own. But before I let you in on what that skill is and how you can gain it, I want to get a monumental trait out of the way. Without it, you aren't going to get very far, and success in any area of your life will always feel like a distant, unattainable dream.

This trait, a positive attitude, is going to shape the way you interact with people, connect with them, and find joy in almost every moment. In fact, having an optimistic attitude is so powerful that your life depends on it. No, seriously, I mean it. Improving your attitude and outlook on life can not only potentially add years to it,[6] but it will make those years feel more fulfilling – guaranteed.

I'll be the first person to advocate against toxic positivity. That's not my approach here. But authentic positivity does have a lot of weight in finding joy and peace in life. In reality, what you focus on, you will notice more.

Just think about it. If your mind is attuned to finding problems, all you will see is problems. But if you can train yourself to notice the wholesome, positive, and good things in life, you will see how abundant they really are.

The most important thing I need you to know about your attitude is that it's a choice. Yes, whether you have a negative or a positive attitude, it's your choice.

THE IMPORTANCE OF POSITIVITY

A positive attitude is often the deciding factor that swings the pendulum of your reputation. People love someone who can communicate effectively because they uplift the atmosphere and inspire positive emotions in others.

But if you're a pessimistic person, gossiping about people, complaining about the state of the world, and nagging people to get what you want out of them, you'll run into problems. Like clockwork, people will lose interest in you.

Don't get me wrong, an interest in worldly issues is not a bad thing. However, unless you have a constructive opinion to offer, nobody needs another person repeating the same old negative jargon circulating society like "Inflation is really getting out of hand" or "We only have so many years before climate change destroys us."

What I want you to understand about people and the draw of communicating effectively is that hope often feels rare in today's world. Humanity has a terrible reputation in a lot of ways. But experiencing someone who truly *sees* and *understands* you can confirm your deepest beliefs and desires, that there *is* hope for humanity, relationships, and connection.

I know there is a lot constantly going wrong across the globe, but you need to remind yourself that whether you believe it or not, there is so much going right. Even in the depths of war, famine, and social crisis, there is always a possibility for things to improve – and they usually do eventually, but often not without a little hope.

I'd argue that every time humanity saw its way through a global crisis, it wasn't by giving up and accepting our fate. Thanks to the optimists, the fighters, and those who believed in something better, we have made it through it all. Those people who pull us through hard times, whether great leaders or everyday people, all have optimism in common. They believe so fiercely in their optimistic vision that they don't give up until it's a reality. Those people are the ones hopeful enough to lead the way and turn a crisis into an opportunity to triumph. Optimism is powerful like that.

You see, you can't communicate effectively without a positive attitude. It's difficult to persuade people to trust you, follow you, or like you without optimism. Society sees optimism as superior in so many ways. And it's not wrong.

Some benefits of adopting an optimistic point of view include:

- Resilience
- Persuasiveness
- Increased likability

Take notes! This is important.

Resilience: When you can consistently see the silver lining in any situation, you won't give up as easily as someone who never sees a way out of their struggles. You can handle confrontation and negativity much more readily as your self-worth and emotional intelligence are greater with an optimistic viewpoint. Plus, a positive attitude generally accompanies a growth mindset, allowing you to see problems as opportunities for growth rather than leaving you feeling bitter and unhappy.

Persuasiveness: The way people perceive you will differ significantly if you have an optimistic outlook on life compared to a pessimistic one. This is because of a few things: rarity, effect, and influence.

You should know that optimism is much rarer than pessimism, especially the optimism that draws people in. Blind optimism, although still optimism, won't necessarily be appealing because anyone with a pessimistic mindset will see right through it.

To be persuasive in your communication, you need to have the kind of optimism to acknowledge the negativity in the world without letting it affect your attitude. This means being able to expect the best out of life while being prepared for the worst. You'll never be blindsided or seen as biased this way, rather an attractive force of endearing influence toward positivity.

Because effective communicators have such a positive outlook on life without ignoring the negatives, their outlook feels refreshing and validating. It positively affects people rather than selfishly putting them down for having a different view.

This kind of optimism inspires positivity in others, which can benefit you. For example, people are far more likely to do a favor for someone positive and kind over someone who is pessimistic and rude. That's influential. I'm not saying pessimistic people can't be kind, but pessimism often breeds negativity in others, while optimism breeds positivity.

Increased likability: The more optimistic and joyful you are, the more likable you will be.

Optimism increases likability by creating an aura around you that shines like a light for people in a dark place. So many of us are thirsty for positivity in a world of dreary news headlines and miserable people. Being positive is an easy way to attract and influence people in a way that benefits everyone.

So what are you waiting for?

Are you going to let go of negative beliefs in the pursuit of finding more joy in life and creating it? Are you ready to risk being seen as naive by pessimists for the chance to inspire others with a unique and uplifting point of view? And, are you prepared to put in the effort it takes to release old ways of thinking and behaving to allow your influence to fully set in and shine?

Remember, effective communication takes an optimistic view of life. People who communicate effectively know how to remind us about humanity's triumphs. They're the people who point out how beautiful a storm is rather than waiting for the sunshine. But the catch is, it's all a choice. Now make yours.

HOW TO ADOPT A POSITIVE ATTITUDE

Your attitude will be the basis for your success in building effective communication. Actually, it will be the basis of your success in almost every area of your life.

To shift it is going to take work. It will take courage and trust in the methods I'm about to share with you. But if you're ready and willing, I ask you now to trust, be prepared to take action, and keep reading. These are the steps you need to take to build a positive attitude.

Step 1: Practice Gratitude

Gratitude is not about invalidating your struggles. Practicing gratitude can give you perspective on how big your problems really are. It's okay to feel hurt or stressed when things are going wrong in your life, but the better you get at noticing and focusing on the things you're grateful for, the more strength you'll find to carry on through tough times.

Practicing gratitude is one of the best ways to bring the good in your life to light. We often go about our lives fixated on our problems. That makes us focus on what we *don't* have rather than what we *do*. Gratitude is simply remembering to take a moment and be thankful for those things we neglect to notice.

Take a moment to write down what you've got to be grateful for. In your Workbook, you will find a gratitude exercise waiting for you. Do that exercise now, and then do it every morning or evening from here on out. Share your gratitude in the LearnWell Community for added encouragement. It only takes 5 minutes to practice gratitude. Stay committed to shifting your mindset and see gratitude as a welcomed habit that will change your life.

Another way to uplift your life with gratitude is to simply acknowledge when things go your way. For example, if you're late for the train, but you get there and manage to climb on in time, whisper to yourself, "Thank you" and send that thanks out into the universe. For what it's worth, regardless of what you believe, giving thanks in any way will have a positive effect on you and your life. Remember, the more you feed your focus into something, the more you see it. So tune your mind into seeing the good things in life and be grateful.

Step 2: Challenge Negative Beliefs

Without a positive attitude, shifting your energy and communicating joy authentically is nearly impossible. Practicing gratitude will help train your mind for positivity, but if you don't take the time to deal with the negativity deep within yourself, it might take a while before you truly change for the better.

We all have negative traits and patterns we're not always proud of. It's only human. But to communicate effectively, you need to gain an almost magical sense of self-acceptance. That comes from embracing both the light and the dark about yourself. Keep working on your self-awareness to help you pick up on your negative patterns and false beliefs.

Once you can confidently acknowledge your negative beliefs and patterns, you can work to shift them for the better. Your dark side is flexible. Don't ever think it's reasonable to say, "Oh, this is just who I am." Being rigid against positive change doesn't serve anyone. Find the strength to face your negative beliefs and patterns, question their validity, and work towards shifting them.

You can shift your negative thoughts, beliefs, and patterns with something I like to call conscious reframing, more commonly known as cognitive reframing. This is where you decide that you're going to consciously change your thoughts or "rethink" them in a better way. It's as easy as noticing a negative thought or belief and correcting yourself. This can look like shifting:

- "Everyone's always judging me" to "I often feel judged no matter who I'm around. Maybe my confidence is lacking. What I think of myself is more important than what others think."

- "I don't fit in at work" to "I haven't found where I fit in yet. Maybe I need to get to know more people."

- "People suck" to "It's true there are a lot of people caught up in a pessimistic mindset, but there are also so many amazing people out in the world doing great things."

Challenge your negative thoughts and beliefs. Question if they're overexaggerations, catastrophizations, or generalizations. Adjust your thinking to suit a more objective narrative rather than letting your mind run wild and form unfair, biased beliefs.

So much of a positive attitude is rooted in the way you think. So, don't let your mind get away with thinking in a pessimistic tone. Use conscious reframing to actively choose to think in a more constructive manner.

Step 3: Share In Other People's Joy

Nothing saps the joy out of a positive occasion like envy. Being jealous of someone else's happiness or success not only brings other people down but robs you of joy, too. What's worse is the more time you spend pondering over why other people are happy or successful, and you're not, the more time you take away from your efforts to build happiness and success for yourself. Envy is a massive waste of time.

One of the most endearing things about magnetic people, is they know how to be happy for others. They not only cheer others on and uplift them even more, but they find joy and fulfillment in other people's success and happiness. If you open your eyes, you'll see that sharing in other people's joy is a free ticket to more happiness for yourself – without doing anything.

Instead of allowing people's joy to spotlight your lack thereof, join in! Don't save your empathy to only support people when they're down. Use it to support people when they're up, too. It's as simple as being happy for others. You're happy because they're happy.

Step 4: Don't Let Failure Hold You Back

One of the fundamental differences between pessimistic people and optimistic people is their mindsets. Pessimistic people have a lack mindset, while optimistic people have a growth mindset.

A lack mindset is when you see the world as a place of lack. There isn't enough money to go around. There aren't enough resources. There's too much pollution and crime, and there's nothing you can do about it.

A growth mindset is seeing the world as a place of abundance. There is an opportunity at every corner. There is enough to go around so long as it's managed properly. Yes, there's too much pollution and crime, but everyone can make a difference with effort.

Effective communicators have a growth mindset.

What coins each mindset their names are the contrasting viewpoints regarding challenges and success. This is where I want you to put your focus. People with a lack mindset see failure as a loss. While people with a growth mindset see failure as an opportunity to grow. Remember how Anna reacted even though we never won the hockey match? She used her incredible attitude to see past the struggle and feel proud of what we *did* achieve rather than fixate on what we didn't.

It's okay to feel disappointed when something doesn't go your way, but I urge you to pick yourself up quickly when you fall. You must see setbacks as temporary challenges and *know* better times will always come. Optimism makes failure feel valuable. It is. Use your failures to learn and grow as a person. Never let failure hold you back.

Step 5: Celebrate Often, Even The Little Things

Now, for the fun part. Who said birthdays, weddings, and graduations are the only things worth celebrating? I want you to celebrate the small things, too. There is much to look forward to, embrace, and celebrate. It's time you start noticing that and allowing yourself to revel in the big and little things as often as possible.

Just cooked a lasagna for the first time without burning it? Celebrate! Went to a meeting and spoke in front of the whole team? Amazing! Helped an elderly stranger cross the street? Good on you! Take note of your wins, no matter how small they are. Give yourself a little credit for the good you do, and you might be motivated to do more.

You can celebrate the good in your life and your successes in many ways. For something minor, acknowledgment will do, but as you move on to celebrate more, make a point of it. Appreciate yourself. Treat yourself to something nice. Make a bit of a fuss over your successes. The better you feel about yourself and notice your wins, the more you prime your mind to notice wins for everyone else and for many occasions.

Your optimism is all about feeling more positive in yourself, but it's also about allowing that positivity to become infectious. Share it. Double it. And don't let anyone tell you it makes you weak or naive.

Your attitude will shape and influence every interaction you ever have in life. It will affect your willingness to empathize with others and either block or help further your connections. It's going to impact every other trait you build throughout this book, either hindering your progress or helping it.

I know it's not easy to shift such a fundamental part of yourself but make an effort to see that the change is worth it. To help you see that more fully, this next trait, listening, is one of the traits of effective communication most impacted by your attitude. It shows empathy in its full and truest form. As simple as listening seems, I invite you to read on with an open mind and allow me to deepen your perspective.

8

A RARE AND HIGHLY VALUABLE SKILL

The Impact Of Great Listening Skills And How To Listen Effectively

"Listening is an art that requires attention over talent, spirit over ego, others over self."

– Dean Jackson

TRAIT 5: LISTENING

Subtly ripping up a paper napkin on the table, I smiled at the waitress as she brought out the bottle of red wine we ordered. Mika had just graduated, and Ashley and I decided to take her for our favorite "girl's night" outing; a bottle of wine (or two) and the pizza special at Luigi's Pizzeria.

The waitress poured the wine into our three glasses already set on the table.

There seemed to be a veil over Mika as she spoke excitedly about her degree and the upcoming ceremony. All I could hear was the rising sound of glasses clinking, unsettling bursts of laughter, and the upbeat mandolin playlist that was part of the restaurant's Italian theme. I was starting to feel overwhelmed as my anxiety intensified.

Casually taking a sip of my wine, I did my best to conceal how I felt and focused on making sure Mika knew I was listening. I smiled, nodded to show my interest, and tried to drown out the noise of the restaurant. As usual, Ashley was caught up on her phone, texting her boyfriend and checking her emails.

As Mika went on to tell me about her final exam and receiving her results, I continued my efforts to actively listen to Mika. But even though I was selling enjoyment, I wasn't feeling comfortable at all. I took another sip.

By the third sip, I felt a slight prick of warmth reach my cheeks. The noise from the restaurant slowly became bearable as the numbness of alcohol started to shift me.

Soon, I began loosening up in conversation. This was the Serina my friends knew so fondly and were waiting to see. I started leaning into the topic and asking questions that sparked Mika to reply with such enthusiasm the energy at the table grew. Ashley put her phone down.

For the rest of the night, the three of us laughed wildly and talked about plans, partners, and other relevant things in our lives. I felt present, even though the wine was starting to make the rest of the room blur slightly with each turn of my head. I could be myself. Or at least more of the person I wanted to be.

Ashley and Mika got up for the restroom together and left me to watch our table and handbags. Holding a piece of pizza in my hand, I smiled to myself about the fun I was having. Then a thought crept in as if it was always there but somehow ignored – "Why can't I *always* be like this?"

I wanted the ease of communication I felt under the influence to last! And I was determined to know how. Along with my research, I quickly realized something. Although I could appear to listen very well, even in the midst of chaos, the key change that took place after a glass of wine was the intensity of my intrigue. Without the anxiety there to distract me, I could be more present and listen more deeply. Without that extra layer of inhibitions, I stopped listening with my head and started listening with my heart.

As you've seen, you can know all the right strategies to *show* that you're listening; you can even fool other people into *believing* you're a great listener, but unless you do what I teach you in this chapter, being seen as a great listener is not going to make you effective in communication. And I'm certainly not going to recommend using alcohol as a social lubricant in your pursuit of magnetism. Remember, you can't fake energy. So, let me explain.

LISTENING WITH YOUR HEART

Although communication technically only has two parts, verbal and nonverbal communication, listening is the missing link that creates connection.

Let me repeat that: Listening is the missing link that creates connection.

But even listening is misunderstood. Most books, research, and speakers teaching listening talk about active listening having two parts: Hearing and comprehension. This is where you not only hear what someone is saying, but you actively comprehend their words to respond appropriately.

I want to add something to this active listening equation.

It's something that *I* was missing, even though I had researched and learned how to actively listen to people. I knew all about how to use the right body language, ask the right questions, and make sure the other person felt heard. But I still wasn't fully present in conversations. I was simply practicing a rehearsed display of listening that I knew people responded well to.

You already know that you need to work on your attitude before you can communicate effectively and draw people in. But there's a reason you need to do that. It's something I haven't mentioned yet, but it's what every truly effective communicator knows how to do. You need to lead with your heart rather than your mind. Let me rephrase that.

To communicate effectively, you need to let your heart guide you and not the biases, false beliefs, and doubts of your mind.

Your mind can be very misleading, basing its decisions on the past or a fear of the future. But your heart makes its decisions based on empathy. That's why simply applying the rules of active listening doesn't always work. You must take a heart-led approach. That's what *real* listening is. It's listening with good intentions rather than selfish ones.

What you hope to gain from people matters. If you have people fooled into thinking you're a great friend because you listen so intently, but inside, you're not present or genuine, eventually, your relationships will feel unfulfilling.

I want you to build authentic, genuinely successful relationships that last a lifetime. Or, if you're seeking to communicate more effectively as a form of influence over people, I want you to make an impact and build a reputation that withstands rumors, distance, and time. Use the strategies in this chapter to help you do that.

WHY LISTENING MATTERS

Learning to listen with your heart has a lot of power in conversation. If you can enter a conversation with the intent of being present, authentic, and willing to connect, then you will always have the upper hand.

A Rare And Highly Valuable Skill

I know it might seem like a contradiction, having the right intentions to give you the upper hand, but effective communication is all about finding the balance between give and take. Remember, magnetic people make everyone feel like the winner, including themselves. Having empathy and listening with your heart doesn't mean being completely selfless. It means knowing how to put your doubts aside to both give and gain the most out of an interaction.

You're not here to become the world's best people-pleaser. You're here because you want to make a powerful impact on people and not only improve their lives, but your own as well. You've already done so much work on yourself to put your ego aside and show up with empathy and self-awareness. Now, I want you to use what you've learned to engage with people and truly connect.

Learning how to listen with genuine intentions and love for people will allow you to lead every conversation you enter. Your attention to detail will help you remember names, learn valuable information about people, and give you the confidence to navigate any conversation in the most positive direction.

The better you can listen to someone, show them empathy, and respond in a way that nurtures trust and understanding, the more you will uplift them and build rapport. Without trust and rapport, you won't experience the deep connections you need.

Make sure you're not making my mistake. I don't want you to enter conversations putting on a show of great listening and magnetism to be liked for your own personal gain or to negate fears. You must be authentic in your desire to connect and uplift the interaction. Let your focus be on listening with your heart to form valuable connections for both parties. Don't throw yourself aside. Rather, find a balance between knowing you will benefit from conversations and listening with an authentically caring energy using your empathy.

HOW TO LISTEN

There is a reason you needed to work on your attitude before reading this chapter. Without a positive attitude, you won't be able to listen with your heart. You might be able to hear and comprehend what someone is saying – aka actively listen to them – but unless you genuinely care and *want* to understand someone, you won't be able to truly listen.

People who communicate effectively know how to fully engage and lead the conversation in a positive direction. They connect with people instantly and remember important details about them that can help them further engage and connect again in the future. They know the value of authentic connections, and they listen to everyone with care and love.

I still want you to be able to make someone *feel* heard with active listening. The only difference here is that I want you to take active listening to a more authentic level.

Now that your positive attitude is growing, I know you're ready to connect with people more deeply in conversation. To help you do that, here are a few things you need to consider to become an exceptional heart-lead listener:

What Good Listening Looks Like

With your attitude in check, you need to learn and apply all the principles of active listening. The first thing you need to do to make sure you deepen your connections is *show* people that you care.

Active listening involves using your nonverbal communication skills to influence how someone feels. You need to focus far more on showing someone you are listening rather than telling them.

Make use of everything you learned in Chapter 6, including your body language, tone of voice, and facial expressions. This can look like:

- Open body posture
- Leaning slightly forward
- Reassuring head nods
- Soft smiling
- Appropriate facial reactions
- Comforting gestures and touch
- Kind, even tone of voice

You want to steer clear of any sort of over-the-top nonverbal communication to make sure people feel comfortable around you. But you also don't want to appear emotionless and uncaring. Try to find a balance that feels both warm and comfortable yet confident.

You want to portray positive nonverbal communication signs, even when the person you're speaking to feels low. Show your empathy loud and clear, but make sure you don't allow someone else's energy to sway you too much. Stay stable in yourself, and try to lead any conversation you enter towards a more positive outcome. Showing empathy and listening with intent is powerful enough to diffuse the most heated arguments. So use it to your advantage.

Remember, this won't work for long if your attitude isn't optimistic. Your microexpressions and physical reactions will always give your true emotions and intentions away eventually. Make sure your head and heart are in the right place before engaging with people.

Your Listening Filters

Your subconscious, as well as conscious perspectives about a person, will either help or hinder your connection. This perspective is usually determined by a range of beliefs and experiences involving that person. These act as filters to your understanding of them, directly impacting how well you listen to them.

Some more things that can act as a filter between your perspective and heart-led listening include your values, language, culture, attitude, and intentions. These filters affect the way you see the world and judge other people. If your attitude isn't based on love and understanding, your filters could act as a block.

I need you to become aware of the way your filters influence your connections. Go to your Workbook now and put your filters down on paper. Start with your values, and go on to explain how your language, culture, and intentions might be standing in your way of connection.

It's okay to have filters, differences are not a bad thing. However, if you find your filters creating a bias against certain groups of people, now is your chance to revisit your filters and shift them from a place of human understanding and empathy.

Your filters are closely linked with your belief system, nurtured over a lifetime of experiences paired with your upbringing. If you find yourself feeling blocked by them, go back to Chapter 7 and work through the five steps of a positive attitude again. Realigning your attitude to come from a place of love and understanding will help you work through biases and blocks.

Remember, empathy is a powerful connection tool. Use it to put yourself in someone else's shoes and gain a new perspective so you can move past old beliefs.

The Power Of Silence

Most of us are caught up in the power of great communication skills. But if you can be comfortable in complete silence with a stranger, that shows true social confidence. Mastering an awkward silence is one of the easiest ways to instill trust in someone and communicate leadership. But how do you do that?

I'll keep referring back to it mercilessly because it is so important – empathy. Empathy is your key to exceptional listening and connection building. You can use empathy to read a person correctly and adjust your nonverbal communication to communicate comfort and understanding with them. If you can make someone feel comfortable in your presence without saying a single word, that's effective communication.

The Most Important Part

If you haven't already caught on, empathy and listening are closely linked, if not united. So I want to use what you learned about empathy to explain the difference between being a good listener and being a great one.

Remember, empathy has three parts: putting yourself in someone else's shoes, understanding *their* point of view, and adjusting your behavior to accommodate them. The same goes for listening. You can hear what someone is saying, fully comprehend and care, but fail to positively affect the way they feel.

To completely influence and impact someone, you have to hear and comprehend what they're saying, then adjust how you respond accordingly. Yes, using your nonverbal communication skills is a powerful way to do this, but this is one of the occasions where what you say and how you reply matters a lot.

Just because verbal communication only makes up 7% of your conversation doesn't mean it's not important. In many ways, what you say will be the reactant that sways the conversation one way or another.

It's easy to show someone that you genuinely care on the surface but to break beyond that and reach greater depths of connection and impact, you need to play an active role in any conversation.

You know how to hear and comprehend what someone is saying. Now you need to apply what you've absorbed to your responses. As you learned in Chapter 5, asking questions can help show how much you care and how well you listen. Tie that chapter in as your final step to listening with your heart.

Ask questions that influence the person in a positive way. What you say and how you say it will either help someone open up or make them want to shut down. Stay in tune with them and practice replying in different ways and with different words to notice what helps people feel regulated, understood, and ready to open up more.

For example, one of the most affirming things you can do during conflict or conversation is simply repeat back what you hear. You can either frame this as a statement to show your understanding, or you can frame it as a question and influence elaboration. This can sound like, "I see you are passionate about your parenting style?" or "It sounds like it really upsets you when people question your parenting style?"

Asking affirming questions is a common conflict-resolution tactic, but you can use it to establish a deeper connection with someone regardless of the conversation topic or tone. It leaves room for the person to either confirm that you've understood them and elaborate or correct you and reveal even more about themselves.

Learn To Focus

Finally, the last thing you need to do as a heart-led listener is learn to stay focused during conversation. Luckily, if your attitude is in the right place and you genuinely *want* to understand people, staying focused is easy.

However, sometimes a desire to listen isn't enough. How well you stay focused and present around people can determine how magnetic they find you. If you're constantly getting distracted or losing track of the conversation, you're not going to get very far with most people.

The easiest way to help yourself focus and feel drawn into conversation with someone is to, firstly, remove distractions like cellphones or TV, and secondly, find common ground with them. If you are not interested in the person or the conversation, it could be hard to maintain the level of engagement and connection you're after.

But, if you can't do that, there is a final failsafe to connect with almost anyone in almost any situation – be curious.

Sometimes, finding reasons to understand someone is difficult, especially when you're not looking to gain a relationship with that person, be it friendship, romantic, or professional. So, instead of seeing every conversation as an opportunity to gain a relationship, I want you to consider what else you can gain from positive connections with people.

Think about what you can learn or how you can benefit the person. There's always something to give and gain from every interaction you have. Even conflict can teach you something valuable. Again, empathy can help you channel your interest and find a desire to know more in order to actively listen to anyone.

But now that you know how to apply listening skills to your pursuit of effective communication, I want to deepen the discussion of curiosity and dive into two more vital habits associated with connected people. Let's shift our focus from solid traits you need to build to the three habits of effective communication that will help set every other trait in stone.

9

3 HABITUAL APPROACHES YOU NEED

How To Reestablish Your Passion For Life And Prioritize Joy

"Fun is one of the most important and underrated ingredients in any successful venture."

– Richard Branson

TRAIT 6: CIA

There are three habits most children have that make them innocently vibrant and endearing. They're also the three things that become tainted with the negativity that tends to weed its way into our minds as we mature. They're the three habits that great communicators have mastered to experience life with the most enchanting and infectious happiness. They are curiosity, intelligence, and authenticity.

CURIOSITY

Curiosity is all about having an interest in things, often a wide variety of things. It's about caring to learn something new, expanding your perspectives, and understanding things you haven't figured out yet.

We spoke about curiosity in Chapter 8 and how it can help you forge beautiful and mutually beneficial connections through the art of heart-lead listening. Think about what you learned in the previous chapter, and consider how much more you might be missing out on without curiosity.

Without a curious mind, you stay closed off to new possibilities, information, and experiences. You might feel like you have nothing more to learn or feel like there's no point in it. But, this is where you must become merciless in your quest for vibrancy. If you don't start practicing curiosity across the board, how can you expect to see that there *is* more to life than what you've been living?

The only way to reveal the beauty of life that is hiding in plain sight is to become open to it. Curiosity becomes a window allowing you to see what negativity rendered invisible. If you allow yourself to become curious, you will start to see the world as a place with more to offer you. So, make curiosity a part of who you are by practicing it until it becomes a habit.

Like you did when you were a child, question everything. Look upon the world with fresh eyes because every moment of life is new. You are never living the same moment twice, so what makes you think that you know what's about to come next?

Stop trying to predict and project what you think onto situations, circumstances, and conversations. Use your curiosity to face every moment with a sense of wonder and interest to learn more than you could ever imagine. With curiosity, every moment becomes an opportunity to understand life better.

To make curiosity a habit, try:

- Entertaining small talk with curiosity rather than contempt.
- Becoming open to the unknown rather than fearing it.
- Trying new things without judgment.
- Pretending to do something for the first time to experience it with fresh eyes.
- Diving into discussions about topics you know nothing about.

If you are curious and interested, you become interesting. People are drawn to seekers. It's obvious when someone looks at the world with an open mind, willing to indulge in new information and experiences. If you are curious, everything about you will open up. Your body language becomes open, your eyes sparkle with intrigue, and your energy draws information out of people.

That's where the second habit comes in. Once you are curious, you need to be willing to do what comes next. You can't just observe the information you notice. You need to absorb it like a sponge and let it change you for the better.

INTELLIGENCE

One of the things that is often thrown around throughout school is our IQ and intelligence. If you're not good at maths, it doesn't matter how great you are at art, you might still feel that you are not as intelligent as the people getting A+'s on every algebra quiz. You might feel like your efforts are better spent out on the track or in home economics. Or, you might feel like you're better off staying at home than spending another day in school feeling like a failure.

Whatever your idea of intelligence and IQ is, put it aside for a moment. You need to know that no matter what your report cards looked like, it is not necessarily a reflection of your intelligence. Intelligence has far more to do with your thirst for knowledge than your ability to memorize textbooks and ace tests.

For this habit, you need to use the curiosity you've practiced and take it a step further into action. Don't stop at becoming more open to new experiences and knowledge. Actively start to pursue them and absorb what you learn like a sponge.

Take the things you learn and see what you can apply to your life to make it better. Use your experiences to grow as a person and develop a powerful character. Effective communicators have a strong presence and personality. Building your intelligence will help you gain those things.

Here's how you can increase your intelligence:

- Read or listen to books frequently, even daily.
- Engage in interesting conversations with interesting people and ask questions.
- Pay attention to the world around you and learn from experience.
- Practice problem-solving rather than seeking answers online for every problem.
- Swap reality TV for documentaries and podcasts.
- Engage in online communities dedicated to learning like the LearnWell Community.

However, to gain a well-rounded intelligence, I don't want you to stop at IQ. EQ, in other words, your emotional intelligence, is just as important, if not more important. Your EQ is the form of intelligence that allows you to make a positive emotional impression on people. It's how you use your empathy to be authentic and vulnerable in everything you do. Without EQ, your social and emotional connections will suffer. Make an effort here, and take notes.

AUTHENTICITY

I've mentioned this to you before, but it's worth reiterating. Communicating effectively doesn't mean becoming someone you're not. Magnetically connected people, like most children, are unapologetically themselves. They are never afraid to be authentic, even if it means being vulnerable.

Vulnerability is a sign of emotional intelligence. If you are able to accept yourself to the degree that you are comfortable and capable of sharing your true feelings, you're not weak. You're incredibly powerful. Why? Because there is no better way to reach another person than to be relatable, honest, and willing to put your ego aside.

You can't be the most authentic version of yourself if you aren't comfortable being vulnerable. Like a dog that rolls onto its back, happy to reveal its vital organs for a tummy scratch, vulnerability shows that you trust someone with your weak spots. It shows that you are open to getting to know someone on a deeper level, and it creates a space for people to draw closer and authentically connect with you in return.

When you become so comfortable in yourself that you move through life with authenticity, you instantly attract connection. Authenticity is one of the most attractive habits you can build, and it is the final child-like habit that will bring your passion for life back in full swing.

You can become more authentic by:

- Getting to know yourself.
- Accepting the parts of yourself that you can't change.
- Pursuing personal development to become a happier person.

- Sharing your genuine and true feelings with people.
- Releasing the need to be perfect in private or public.
- Respecting your own values and boundaries.

People who communicate effectively aren't out in the world rigidly going about life. They're the people yearning for more, seeking, and exploring. They don't care about the status quo. They put joy above what other people think of them and their ideals. They know life is incredible, and they allow themselves to live it fully.

I know there is a lot that can stand in your way, especially if you struggle with mental health. But, to communicate effectively and become the authentic person you're here to become, you need to be willing to face parts of yourself you may not like. You need to step up and let go of any insecurities you have so you can exist in the world with confidence in who you are. Go to your Workbook now and reflect on ways you can bring more joy into your life with curiosity, intelligence, and authenticity.

Nobody will fully accept and embrace you if you can't do that for yourself. So, let's move on to Chapter 10 where you'll face your insecurities and start walking through life with the confidence of the most magnetic version of yourself. You can't be confident to your core if you won't let go of the things holding you back. It's time to turn the page and unshackle yourself.

Note: Give yourself a great pat on the back! You have officially passed the halfway mark of your 7-day journey to effective communication. But don't stop now... Process everything, practice what you can, and come back tomorrow for Day 5.

10

A FOUNDATION OF CONFIDENCE

How To Build Confidence
From The Ground Up

"Believe in your infinite potential. Your only limitations are those you set upon yourself."

– Roy T. Bennet

TRAIT 7: CONFIDENCE

If you were to combine every trait of effective communication you've learned so far, but leave out these next two, you might still get a person who is interesting and kind, but would they be truly magnetic?

No.

Like a gift, all the traits up until this point have been about substance – what's inside. This chapter is all about the wrapping paper – your confidence to openly share what a gift you are. And the final trait, which I'll reveal soon, is the bow that ties it all together – the cherry on top.

This is where it's time to bring back the topic we spoke about in Chapter 2, your perceived attractiveness. Confidence directly impacts the way people perceive you. So much of attraction – magnetism – is about your presence and how you express yourself to the world. You've already been working on that.

You've worked on your self-awareness and getting to know exactly who you are and who you want to be. You've practiced putting yourself in others' shoes and changing your behavior to accommodate anyone in any situation using empathy. Your energy and attitude are bright and infectious. Listening has become a heartfelt experience, and your zest for life is returning with curiosity, intelligence, and authenticity.

But the problem is, it doesn't matter how much substance you hold inside. If you don't feel confident expressing that substance to the world, your value won't be perceived accurately. If your wrapping paper communicates a valuable gift, but all that's inside is packing peanuts, people are going to be disappointed. But you can be the most valuable gift in the world if you're wrapped up in a paper bag. Although, you're not doing yourself any favors.

I know you've worked really hard to become the most effective communicator you've ever been. With that effort, you are ready to wrap your foundation in the most dazzling display you can find by learning to express yourself with confidence.

You've already done so much work to get to know yourself and become a more vibrant person, but there's still one thing standing in your way – insecurities.

We all have them.

However, the difference between most people and those with incredible communication skills is this: They aren't afraid to face their insecurities. That's what you have to do, right now. If you want to walk through life with unshakable confidence and dazzling charisma, you must be willing to confront your insecurities and do something about them.

Insecurities are loud. Even if you try as hard as you can to outshine them, they'll always find a way to dampen you. Working through any insecurities you may have will allow you to either dissolve them or embrace them. It's only natural to have flaws. To communicate effectively is not to be perfect, but rather to wear your imperfections with confidence and self-acceptance.

Part of knowing yourself means understanding your insecurities and working with them rather than trying to avoid them. Once you can comfortably face your insecurities as they come up, confidence will come with ease. You can't skip ahead and try to work on your confidence when you haven't bothered to consider why you're not confident to begin with.

So, I'm going to give you 3 exercises you must do right now before moving on. They will not only make confidence come naturally but reveal valuable information about yourself. The better you know yourself, the more opportunity you have to love yourself fully. And when you love and accept yourself fully, nobody can bring you down.

FACING INSECURITIES

Before we get to the exercises, let's talk about where insecurities come from. If you were born in a vacuum, you might never feel insecure about anything. But, from the moment you open your eyes for the first time, you are affected by external influences of all kinds. You're faced with the opinions and pressures of the world and the influence of your experiences.

For example, growing up with copious teen magazines and the rise of social media gave me a well of ideals to feel pressured by, particularly with my looks. It only took a year after puberty to develop an eating disorder and body dysmorphia. But remove the heavily edited photographs and toxic magazine headlines like "Try this water fast to get your summer body overnight!" and I wouldn't have thought there was anything wrong with me, at least not to the extent that I did.

The same goes for *any* insecurities. They spur from false beliefs, false narratives, and a lack of self-love. But find the root of the problem, and you can lift the veil of illusion for yourself. After all, insecurities are rooted in your perspective.

So, the first thing you need to do is realize that you can be wrong about a lot of things. Just because you feel something to be true doesn't mean it is. If you feel like your nose is too big, you've likely compared it to people who feel like their nose is too small.

Of course, insecurities aren't always about appearance. Maybe you've done something you're not proud of and now see yourself as lesser. Maybe something happened to you, and you felt your worth drain out of you. Whatever your insecurities are about, these three exercises will help you acknowledge them, release them, and move forward with grace.

Exercise 1: Challenge The Negative

Since Chapter 4, you've been working on accepting your flaws and getting to know yourself better. Then, in Chapter 7, we spoke about conscious reframing. This exercise is a follow-up of Step 2: Challenge Negative Beliefs. But, instead of reframing your general negative thoughts, I want you to focus on the negative thoughts you have about yourself. These are a direct reflection of your insecurities.

Go to your Workbook now and find the pages dedicated to this exercise. Write down 10 negative thoughts you have about yourself on a regular basis.

Negative thoughts about yourself can look like:

- I'm so embarrassing.
- I'm too fat to wear this outfit.
- Why can't I do anything right?
- I'm a failure.
- I'm never good enough.
- Nobody likes me.
- I don't fit in anywhere.
- I must be the most unlucky person alive.

Next, analyze the thoughts you've written down, and think about what insecurities they associate with. Write down the insecurity you've discovered next to the negative thought. It's okay if some or all of the thoughts are about the same insecurity.

For example, if you often think things like, "I'm such an idiot," "Why can't I do anything right?" or "I should've known better," you might have an insecurity about your intelligence or capability. Maybe you feel incompetent in life. Simply use your thoughts to figure out and acknowledge what your most significant insecurities are.

As you become aware of your insecurities, I want you to question them. Ask yourself whether they are objectively true or not. Circle the ✗ next to the insecurities that are based on false beliefs, and circle the ✓ next to the ones that have some weight. For example, if you feel like a bad friend, ask yourself why you feel that way and if it's true or not. Do that for each insecurity you discover.

Once you have an understanding of your insecurities, you must work on either improving them or releasing them if you want to feel confident. There's no point in allowing insecurities to weigh you down. You have control over them and can choose to either work on them or let them go.

For example, if you're insecure about your nose but you can't do anything realistic to change it. Rather than loathing in the mirror every morning, do the work that it takes to accept your nose as it is and direct your energy toward more important things.

But if you are insecure about being a bad friend or a loner, and you are sure that it's somewhat true, do something about it. Stop wasting your time worrying about all the friends who've cast you aside, and become the friend you've always wished you had. Show up as an amazing friend for people, and you will gain amazing friendships.

That's what will set you apart. People with confidence aren't afraid to face their insecurities. So don't give up now, be brave and do the things most people aren't willing to. Stop shoving your insecurities to the side. Face them, and either accept them or release them.

Exercise 2: Shift Your Focus

Insecurities are ruminations of emotions and thoughts that don't serve you. But, like we spoke about in Chapter 7, the more you focus on negativity, the more you notice it.

If you are too caught up in your failures, you will start to see yourself as someone who always fails. Whichever way you look at it, it's impossible to be a failure 100% of the time. Chances are, you're simply overlooking your wins. But effective communicators know how to recognize a win, even in the smallest situations.

For this exercise, I want you to shift your focus. If you focus on the negative aspects of yourself and your life, it won't be long until you feel negative about who you are. Insecurities will creep in before you know it.

But if you shift your focus onto the things you do right, no matter how small they are, you will naturally start to notice more positivity in your life. You will grow a more balanced perspective of who you are and start to feel happy within your own skin – something fundamentally important for building confidence.

Again, insecurities are based on a skewed perspective about yourself. If you are insecure in any way, shift your focus to balance things out for yourself. To do that, I want to remind you of step 6 in Chapter 7: Celebrate Often, Even The Little Things.

However, for the sake of healing your insecurities, I want you to shift your focus on the positive things that you do. Stop ruminating on your mistakes and rather celebrate your wins. Learn to notice the good that you do, whether it's for yourself or other people.

For example, if you have been eating junk food for a week, instead of beating yourself up and feeling insecure about your bad eating habits, make a change right now and celebrate it. Cook up a healthy meal and praise yourself for making the effort. Not only will you save yourself the pain of shame, but you will feel encouraged to carry on.

The happiest, most magnetic people are kind to themselves. They don't waste time shaming and blaming themselves for mistakes. They acknowledge them, take action towards positive change, and allow themselves to move forward with grace.

Being too hard on yourself often backfires. So, ease up, take responsibility for your actions, and stay focused on your wins. Celebrate them, no matter how small. It's the easiest way to build your self-esteem and kick insecurities to the curb.

Exercise 3: Build Your Self-Love

On the topic of self-esteem, this final exercise for overcoming insecurities is all about self-love. If you can learn to love yourself above anything else in the world, it suddenly becomes very difficult for anyone or anything to bring you down for long.

When I say self-love, I'm talking about the relationship you have with yourself on a deep level. It's not about putting yourself on a pedestal but rather allowing yourself to be your top priority. If you give your energy away to everyone and everything around you before you've even felt worthy of it yourself, you're going to be depleted very soon. But if you love yourself fully and wholeheartedly, your passion for life will return.

It's vital that you make sure you feel strong and confident in yourself before you try to help anyone else. You're so much more valuable to the world at your best. So make sure you love yourself enough to nurture yourself into the strongest and best version.

Insecurities have no place in the heart of someone who has already loved every part of themselves unconditionally. You have to love and accept yourself for all your flaws as well as your strengths. That way, it won't matter what happens to you or who says what about you. Negativity will never be able to linger within you.

To learn to love yourself means to honor your life by taking the best care of both your physical and mental health. Prove to yourself that you matter. Take the necessary steps to nurture your well-being. Let self-care be your greatest tool here.

Self-care that nurtures self-love includes:

- Journaling
- Eating a healthy diet
- Exercising in a way you enjoy
- Spending time outdoors or with animals
- Taking time to rest and relax
- Making time for fun and hobbies
- Asking for help when you need it

I'll leave it up to you to implement the things you know you need to do to make yourself fall in love with life again. If you're working too hard or pushing yourself to the point of failure, take a step back and rest. If you're constantly distracting yourself with TV or social media, take a digital break and spend some time outdoors undistracted. If you've been isolated for some time, reach out to loved ones and enjoy some social interaction.

A Foundation Of Confidence

BUILDING CONFIDENCE

Now that there's less standing in your way, your efforts to build confidence won't be in vain. Your confidence has likely already improved throughout this book, but I want to give you food for thought. What does full-on confidence look like?

Confidence is not about masking nerves with courage so that you appear confident meanwhile you're trembling. It's less about what other people think of you and more about how you feel. It's not a wild display of pageantry to gain attention but rather a calm comfort in any situation.

Let me repeat that: Confidence is comfort in any situation.

Have you ever observed someone with full-on confidence tackling a situation that would normally have you sweating? What did they look like? How did they act? Did they seem calm and comfortable in a situation where you'd normally be terrified? That's confidence.

Yes, doing things that scare you can help you build confidence, but it is not a display of confidence. To truly be confident, you need to grow your comfort in those situations. So, with your insecurities out of the way, pluck up your courage and try these confidence-building exercises so you can express yourself with comfort in any moment.

Exercise 1: Gradual Exposure

I'm starting off your confidence practice with the most daunting exercise there is. Gradual exposure is all about getting out there and facing your fears. It's about doing things that make you uncomfortable to gradually build comfort instead.

To practice gradual exposure, think about situations where you lack confidence. I'm not talking about dangerous situations, but rather situations you know are safe but which activate your stress response.

One at a time, go out and engage in those situations slowly but surely. You don't have to dive right in, just dip in your toe as far as you are able to. It's not about jumping into the deep end and scaring yourself out of trying something again. But rather about gradually allowing yourself to work up to the full experience with confidence.

To make things easier, break down your fears into smaller steps and make an effort to work your way up. Go to your Workbook now, and write down the first fear you want to work on. Then, think about how you can break that fear down into smaller, more manageable goals.

For example, if you are terrified of public speaking, you could break down your goal to become confident on stage like this:

- Write a great speech and practice it in the mirror
- Make your speech in front of a trusted family member
- Practice going up on stage in front of an empty room
- Make your speech in front of a small group of people
- Take your speech onto the main stage in front of a crowd

Once you have broken down your fear into manageable steps, you don't have to do each step only once before moving on. The idea of gradual exposure is to move on to the next step once you have become more comfortable. Practice each step over and over again until you notice your confidence building. Then, once it's no longer as challenging, move on to the next step and repeat.

Gradual exposure is a powerful tool to build trust in yourself and your abilities. As you face your fears and realize that you can do anything you set your mind to, you will feel your confidence soar. Your comfort zone will be expanded, and you can be yourself in more and more situations.

Exercise 2: Practice Positive Self-Talk

Negative thoughts are the worst poison for your mind and confidence. Now that you are comfortable challenging your negative thoughts, you can take it a step further and start practicing positive self-talk instead.

Positive self-talk is all about speaking to yourself with kindness, love, and encouragement. It's about being your own support system and using your inner voice to uplift yourself.

Not only does positive self-talk battle negative thinking, but it also serves as an easy and effective confidence booster. Learning positive self-talk is like becoming your own inner cheerleader, encouraging you through any situation.

There are many ways to practice positive self-talk. Conscious reframing is a great start. But, to help you find the right words

SPEAK EASY

during a tough situation, affirmations are my go-to positive self-talk method.

Instead of simply reframing your thoughts, you teach your mind to think positive, affirming thoughts regardless of whether a negative thought preceded it. The best affirmations are I am statements. They sound like this:

- I am confident
- I am capable
- I am enough
- I am worthy
- I am vibrant
- I am fun
- I am charming

In your Workbook, there is a page dedicated to your affirmations. Use that page to write down 5 affirmations that you are going to repeat to yourself every morning and evening. Whatever affirmations move you and uplift you to becoming more confident, write them down. They can be words that inspire transformation, healing, or excitement about who you are.

When you're done, you can either set a reminder on your phone to read your affirmations straight from your Workbook, or you can pull out the page and stick it on your mirror or anywhere you will see it often.

Exercise 3: Own Your Mistakes

One of the main reasons for a lack of confidence is the fear of messing up in front of other people. You might be afraid of failing, making a mistake, or doing something embarrassing. Before we move on, let's get something very clear. You must question why you are afraid of messing up. Why is your fear of failure holding you back when failure is the best opportunity for growth you can get?

To communicate effectively means to have a growth mindset. You can't allow yourself to be concerned about what people think of you or your mistakes. If you can see your failures as opportunities for growth, in other words, lessons, that's when confidence becomes second nature.

If you struggle with owning your mistakes, go back to Chapter 7 and work on your attitude. You shouldn't be allowing mistakes and failures to govern who you are and how you behave. Pick yourself up, dust yourself off, and learn something. There's always something new to learn.

And as for embarrassment. I know it's difficult to put your ego aside when something happens that makes you feel a bit stupid. Maybe you trip over your own shoelaces or knock over your drink on a first date. Sounds mortifying, doesn't it?

Well, this is where I'm going to reveal the cherry on top of effective communication. Now that you're feeling more comfortable expressing who you are and taking up space as your most authentic self, tie a bow on it by finessing your sense of humor.

There's something amazing about a person who can mess up and laugh at themselves. It's hard not to like someone who isn't afraid of their flaws. People who communicate effectively know how to turn embarrassment into a reminder that life's not that serious. So, learn to laugh a little, even if that means laughing at yourself. And if you really want to use humor to embellish your personality and become magnetic to your core, turn the page to the final chapter of Part 2, and let me show you how a little bit of laughter and smiles can go the distance.

11

LAUGHTER & SMILES

Going The Extra Mile With An Effective Sense Of Humor

"Laughter is the shortest distance between two people."

– Victor Borge

TRAIT 8: HUMOR

Have you ever seen a deep frown disappear from a crying friend's face the minute something funny happens? Maybe you've stubbed your toe and hollered out a string of profanity that made someone close to you laugh, transforming anger into amusement. Have you ever reveled in a funny memory that you can't seem to go long without revisiting? Then you know the value of humor.

Humor is more than being able to crack jokes and make people laugh. A sense of humor runs much deeper than that. Jokes and laughter are merely the symptoms of a great sense of humor. And great communicators know how to use humor as a tool of upliftment – it's simply the cherry on top of effective communication skills.

Anyone can use humor in an attempt to light up another person, but effective communicators are seldom unsuccessful. They know how to deliver their humor in a way that translates accurately for everyone. In this chapter, I will explain how you can do this too.

I want you to develop the kind of humor that takes intelligence. I want you to learn to read the room and adjust your humor to do what it is intended to do – uplift the atmosphere. But that takes apprehension and a sense of what is appropriate and what's not.

It's not called a *sense* of humor for nothing. Humor is a powerful indicator of someone's ability to communicate effectively. It's going to tie everything you've learned together with a nice big bow.

So, with the purest intentions, I want you to listen carefully and remember everything you've learned up until this point. I will break humor down into 8 steps to give you an understanding of how you can be successfully funny, endearing, and comforting in any situation. A good sense of humor is a sign of intelligence, and remember what we said about intelligence in Chapter 9: it's not just about your IQ but also your EQ. So, moving forward, exercise your emotional intelligence whenever you use humor to avoid leaving a bad taste in someone's mouth.

HOW TO EXERCISE AN EFFECTIVE SENSE OF HUMOR

Let me start by clarifying something that extends across all 8 steps to an effective sense of humor. Humor is *never* about putting someone else down to elevate yourself.

Over time, you can dabble with some fun teasing and prodding. But, unless you build a reputation for being a kind and sensitive person, your humor could easily be mistaken. The more you can express your true intentions with people, showing that they are good, the better people will take your jokes.

These 8 steps are going to prime your sense of humor for an effective execution. I want your jokes to land, inspire laughter, and allow people to let go of seriousness to embrace silliness.

Humor is a universal language that can bring people together, even without speaking a word. Remember, humor is not about what you say or do. It's about the joy you can make people feel.

Step 1: Read The Room

The easiest way to make sure you use your humor to attract people towards you is to adapt to the people you're with. Humor is a tool. It's meant to help you connect and uplift. With care and observation, you can steer your humor in a way that makes sense.

Use your receptivity to make an educated assumption about what type of humor will land best in the situation you're in and the people you're around. An easy example is any kind of event that calls for seriousness. If you don't take care to be receptive with your humor, you can quickly tarnish your reputation. You can still apply humor in these circumstances to uplift the energy, so long as you take care to approach the situation with empathy.

To be clear, you should never make jokes about divorce during a wedding, death at a hospital, or any kind of inappropriate jokes at a funeral, if any. There will always be moments where you can slip a little humor into conversation, but the success of your jokes will lie with your receptivity.

To be as receptive as possible in any given situation, read the room. Pay attention to who you're with, use your empathy to gauge how they might be feeling, and make sure your intentions are aligned with the situation at hand.

The more receptive you are to those around you, the quicker you will pick up any hints of humor from them, what their interests are, and their general demeanor. Then, use common sense to decide what humor will be appropriate.

Step 2: Make Sure People Can Read You

As much as it matters for you to read the room, it is equally as important for others to be able to read your intentions accurately. If your intentions are pure and positive, there is a higher chance of your humor translating well. But if your intentions aren't clear, your jokes may cause offense, awkwardness, and dislike.

Of course, you can't fully control the filters through which people see and experience you. But you can ensure you send all the right signals to express your intentions. As we discussed in Chapter 6, you can't fake energy or intentions. Having the right intentions is the first step, but sometimes, we fall into bad nonverbal habits that send the wrong message.

While you build a reputation for being someone who is kind and fun to be around, you must pay attention to your body language cues. Ensure your body language shows that you are calm, comfortable, happy, and open. A positive demeanor will help give your jokes an automatic positive spin.

One of the most obvious and powerful body language cues you need to practice to accurately express your humor is your smile. Focus on becoming someone who smiles easily. If someone makes a joke or funny remark around you, be quick to respond with a genuine smile.

Your smile should translate warmth, comfort, and joy. If you struggle with your smile, practice smiling in the mirror. Think about funny memories or jokes and channel that joy into your smile. Make sure to allow your smile to light up your whole face, especially your eyes, and feel your face transform.

Step 3: Prime Yourself For Laughter

Humor is all in your energy. If you've ever heard someone with an awkward demeanor, tone of voice, and lack of confidence try to land a joke, I'm sure you know it doesn't usually sell. One of the easiest ways to become funnier is to be someone who is comfortable with humor in general. This is someone who is quick on their feet with jokes, laughs easily, and enjoys humor fully.

To become someone comfortable with humor, you must prime yourself for laughter. I want you to open yourself up to humor completely – let laughter into your life.

You can do this by watching more comedies, reading humorous books, enjoying stand-up comedy skits, and anything else that gets you cracking up. If you take life too seriously and feel stiff enjoying humor, people will see you as a stick in the mud. Loosen up and learn to laugh a little.

Step 4: Don't Be Afraid To Be The Butt Of A Joke

Confident communicators aren't quickly offended. Quite the opposite. Remember, as we covered in the previous chapter, they have their insecurities under control. Now that you've put in the work to face your insecurities, I want you to take it one step further. I want you to become so secure in yourself that it doesn't phase you to be the butt of a joke. Better yet, I want you to learn to laugh at yourself.

Self-deprecating humor is not about getting down on yourself about your flaws. It's about owning them. Any time you tease yourself or laugh at your mistakes, it shows people that you are comfortable with yourself, and it inspires others to accept their flaws, too.

Everyone is flawed in one way or another. Don't take yourself too seriously. Use your flaws and mistakes to your advantage and lighten up about them. Tease yourself, chuckle at your silly mistakes, and don't get offended if someone tries to tease or insult you. Flip the script and laugh it off.

Self-deprecating humor is one of the greatest displays of self-assurance. The more people see how comfortable you are teasing yourself in a funny and light-hearted way, the less likely they are to misinterpret your jokes. It's also very difficult to genuinely insult someone who makes light of their flaws so openly. You must get comfortable being the butt of a joke before you attempt to joke about someone else.

Step 5: Teasing With Caution

Even once you have a good reputation for being a funny person, you must always exercise caution when teasing others. Teasing should never be about bringing the other person down. If your jokes cause someone to feel shame in any way, you've failed. There are no excuses for using humor as a weapon.

However, don't negate teasing completely. It can be a great way to deepen your connection with someone, put a positive spotlight on them, or show them that you notice them. The key here is caution. 5 rules to live by for safe and effective teasing are:

- Joke about something light-hearted, never something serious.

- Make the focus something the person is clearly very confident about.

- Save teasing for people you know well unless it's light-hearted.

- Apologize if you accidentally offend someone.

- When in doubt, stick to positive humor.

Always, always, always use empathy to gauge what someone might be comfortable with or not. If you know them well, stay clear of personal jokes in public to avoid exposing them in some way. And if you've just met someone, keep the teasing very positive and light-hearted.

For example, rather than trying to make a joke about the stain on your friend's shirt, try teasing how well they always color code their suit and tie. If your friend trips and falls, tease them about how well they bounced rather than what a clutz they are. If it's someone you just met, you could make a silly joke about your first impression of them, or even better, stick with some self-deprecating humor.

Step 6: Don't Be Predictable

Laughter is easily sparked when we're caught off guard. Use that to your advantage. The human mind is often automatically predicting what someone is going to say next. For example, if I say, "This little piggy went to market, this little piggie…" How would you expect me to finish that sentence? With "stayed home."

To spark laughter in someone, don't be predictable. Use unpredictability to catch people off guard and say something they might least expect. For example, what if I said, "This little piggie went to market, this little piggie became ham." It's silly, but because it's what's least expected and possibly even a little savage, the mind immediately recognizes it as a joke.

Find opportunities to say what's least expected to catch people off guard and make them laugh easily. You can start in small ways first. For example, if you're having a bad day and someone asks how you are, instead of saying, "I'm okay, thanks," you could say something like, "I'm a wreck!" followed by a chuckle. This will likely make the other person smile and lift the energy around you too.

As you become more comfortable with it and more experienced, you'll start to find more opportunities to use it and can experiment with being a little more absurd. You can also play around with how you execute your jokes. However, always read the room to make sure the people you're with are receptive to humor.

Step 7: Accept Failure And Move On Quickly

Sometimes, people aren't receptive to humor. Remember, it takes a *sense* of humor to fully enjoy it. Not everyone has that! Sometimes, your humor won't translate as intended. Rather than letting failure sway you, learn to move on quickly.

In the previous chapter, you practiced 3 exercises to build your confidence. Refer back to those exercises and use them to help you let go of failure like water off a duck's back. And, if all else fails, use self-deprecating humor to point out your mistake and laugh it off.

For example, if you made a bad joke, point out how the joke came out wrong or how terrible it was. If you can own your mistake and tease yourself about it, you give others permission to laugh with you and are less likely to tarnish your reputation.

The better you can handle messing up, using your sense of humor to make light of it, the quicker people will forgive you for a potentially offensive joke. Plus, the more you handle bad jokes or misread rooms with confidence and self-deprecating humor, the more likable you'll be. People will find you relatable.

Step 8: Know How To Respond To Humor

As fun as it is to be funny, recognizing attempts of humor from others will take your communication skills to the next level. But the most important part of recognizing someone else's joke is how you respond to it. You must be able to give others the limelight.

Now that you know how to be funny and how to prime yourself for laughter, use what you've learned to pick up on jokes easily. Then, when you notice someone attempting to make you laugh, engage with it.

You can certainly just allow yourself to laugh, but to inadvertently be the most memorable person in the room, you need to amplify things. Take the joke and piggyback off of it to uplift it and make the person seem even funnier.

Piggybacking on someone's joke is not about stealing the spotlight. It's about rolling with the joke or adding to it. The aim is to stretch the joke's potential. And if you want to make sure this strategy works in your favor, pull all the credit back to the original joker.

With these 8 steps, your humor will do nothing less than magnify the joy waiting to be brought to life all around you. You'll uplift any room you enter, fortify your reputation, and create space for deep, authentic connections to form. In your Workbook, reflect on how you'd like to shift your sense of humor to better communicate who you are. Build your own strategy for humor based on what you've learned.

So long as your intentions are pure, and you do everything you can to communicate those intentions clearly, humor will be the spark that lights up your effective communication skills.

I know how important it is for you to fully embody the communication skills you've learned throughout Part 2. You now know what it means to be authentically magnetic to your bones. As you turn the page to Chapter 12 and start the final Part of this journey, keep what you've learned in mind. In Part 3, you're going to get ample opportunities to practice these 8 traits so that by the end of Chapter 15, they're fully internalized.

Note: This is huge. You've gotten through Parts 1 & 2 in just 5 short days. I hope this has felt more and more rewarding as you've built up your skills. Now there's only one challenge left on this 7-day journey: complete Part 3 in the last 2 days you have. This is going to take determination and a willingness to absorb information like never before. Prepare yourself and come back tomorrow to start Day 6!

PART 3

YOUR CONNECTED LIFE

12

NAILING THE GREETING

Why A Good Greating Is Your Greatest Advantage And How To Execute One

"First impressions die slowly, bad impressions take even longer."

– Joseph Heller

Like a tiered cake of skills, Part 3 is your chance to take every effective communication trait you've acquired up until now and put it to the test. Starting with the simplest yet most important step and ending with the most valuable resource – the foundation for success. These next few chapters are going to challenge you, excite you, and set you up for a life of fulfillment. They're going to establish a system of invaluable skills so you can communicate effectively in any situation forever.

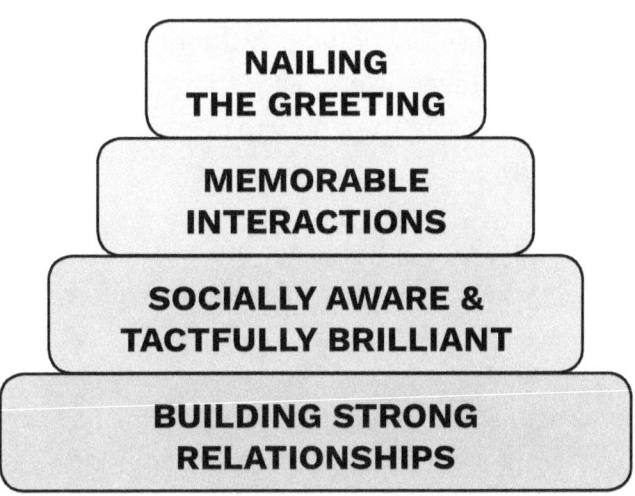

The smallest tier of your connected life – your greeting – is something that sets the tone for the rest of any interaction you'll ever have. Nail this, and you've got your foot firmly planted in the doorway of connection. Your greeting is the first opportunity you have to make a phenomenal impression on someone. Use it wisely, and you're on your way to gaining respect, admiration, and success.

I'm going to give you an unbeatable strategy to nail every greeting you enter. But before you can give an excellent greeting, you need to do three things:

- Exude authenticity
- Get your attitude in check
- Be curious

The energy you enter a greeting with will affect the execution. Make sure you are standing in your authenticity, feel confidently upbeat, and have a level of curiosity that can pull engagement from anyone. If you've forgotten how to do these things, refer back to Chapters 6, 7, and 9.

In short, make sure your intentions are pure when you enter a conversation. If you don't want to be somewhere, it's going to show.

Then, get your thoughts under control and practice constructive thinking. Use your self-awareness to recognize when you're stuck in a negative thinking pattern and cognitive restructuring to remind yourself what thoughts will serve you better. The more positivity you exude, the more you will attract.

Finally, use your curiosity to stay open to new possibilities, information, and experiences. After all, if you're not genuinely curious about who someone is and what they have to say, why would you bother to put effort into your greeting?

Communicating effectively is all about your energy. You must make sure your energy radiates warmth and confidence before worrying about how to bring that through in a greeting. Now that you've brushed up on the three aspects of effective communication above let's move on to putting them into practice from the very start of any interaction.

THE FUNDAMENTALS OF ANY GREETING

Once your energy is vibrant and authentic, you will naturally be more compelling. But if you want to bring your authentic self forth with confidence, this strategy will be your guide:

Step 1: Eye Contact

You can grab someone's attention from across a crowded room with eye contact alone. You can communicate joy, anger, grief, and more without saying a word. Nonverbal communication is the universal language that connects us. And eye contact is the instant link transforming mindless wanderers into momentarily bonded souls. Use it.

Use eye contact to initiate a greeting. Whether it's from a distance or right in front of you, look the person in the eye with intention. Try to keep your eyes a little soft to avoid intensity, but show that you see the person and want to engage with them.

Grip the person in a second or two of deliberate eye contact and move on to step 2.

Step 2: A Smile

Always smile as a reflex to eye contact. Even a stranger could do with a smile! For an excellent greeting, follow your deliberate eye contact with a warm and genuine smile. Use a smile that lights up your face all the way up to your eyes. As we said in step 2 of Chapter 11, your smile should translate into warmth, comfort, and joy. And if you struggle with it, practice in the mirror.

After your initial smile, keep your facial expression comfortable. Your smile and expression will help establish the emotion of the interaction and instill trust. The more your nonverbal communication sends an inviting and comforting message, the more positive the greeting will feel.

Step 3: Touch

Don't overlook the power of touch. As we covered in Chapter 6, touch, also known as haptics, is a powerful communication tool. A simple touch can say many things. In the context of a greeting, use touch to establish trust and connection.

Remember the 5 socially acceptable categories of haptics formulated by researcher R. Heslin? Keep those in mind when gauging what type of touch you will use. However, whatever form of touch you choose for the given situation, let your intentions drive the force of it. If you're trying to comfort, be soft. If you're trying to assert yourself, be firm.

Some examples of touch you can use for each:

- Functional/professional: A good solid handshake.
- Social: A handshake, a shoulder touch, or a hug.
- Friendship: A shoulder touch or a hug.

- Love: A hug and/or a peck.
- Sexual: A kiss.

Of course, these are just examples, and you will need to adjust your greeting for every person you meet. Everyone is different, with their own preferences and comfort zones. Always use your empathy to get a sense of the person you're greeting. It's amazing how much information you can get from observing a person for the few seconds it takes to go up and greet them. Take note of their body language, posture, facial expression, and any other communication cues you can recognize. *Feel* their energy and use your instincts to decide what form of touch will work best.

Step 4: Name Exchange

The next immediate step is vital. Pay attention here. If you have never met someone before, you must be the most open and receptive to absorbing new information during a greeting. Names are extremely important and remembering them is a secret weapon of effective communication – more on this in Chapter 13.

For this step, I want you to say the person's name as you greet them. Don't just say hello, say "Hello, John!" or "Hey, Lily." If it's someone you've never met, introduce yourself and listen out for their name. If they don't automatically reply with their name in return, prompt for it. Whatever you do, never leave a conversation without knowing the person's name.

Some ways you can remember someone's name include:

- Repeat their name back to them: "Hi James, nice to meet you."

- Complement their name: "Ah, Jess is a lovely name."

- Make an association in your mind between them and their name: "Katie with the blue eyes."

- Repeat their name to yourself in your mind.

- When the conversation is over, make a note of it in your phone or journal: "Neighbour from house 27: Pippa."

These 4 steps to an effective greeting will set you up for the memorable interactions that follow. To help paint a picture of how these greetings can go and why they're going to be amazing, let me walk you through some examples.

GREETINGS FOR ANY OCCASION

Sometimes, it's difficult to discern what style of greeting to give for the situation at hand. You don't want to be too casual in a professional setting, and you don't want to be too rigid at a social event. You want to ooze confidence without tilting to arrogance. Let these examples act as a reference for any greeting situation you have to face.

Professional

You enter a meeting and need to introduce yourself. As you walk up to the desk, you make deliberate eye contact and smile lightly. For a professional setting, there is generally no need to overdo

Nailing The Greeting

your smile. Just keep it gentle while allowing it to add warmth to your expression.

As you reach the desk, stand up tall with your shoulders back and reach out your right hand to initiate a handshake if they haven't already. As you shake, keep the tension firm and even without squeezing. You don't want to dominate the handshake. You simply want to use it to confirm your self-confidence.

You can interlace your handshake with a name exchange. Introduce yourself and listen out for their name in return. In this situation, you will likely already know the name of the person you're meeting, but they might not know yours. If you don't know their name, either look out for a nameplate on their desk or ask them for their name in a polite, straightforward way, such as, "Excuse me, but I never got your name?" or "It's great to meet you, Mr/Mrs?"

Nailing a professional greeting will automatically increase your credibility. You will present yourself as someone to be respected and trusted. This type of greeting is all about asserting yourself and showing that you mean business. You're there to put your best foot forward and bring the skills you have to offer to the table. Your greeting can make or break your first impression, so make sure it's a reflection of the reputation you want.

Social

You're invited out for lunch by your friend Susie. Sitting comfortably at the table, you wait for Susie to arrive. When possible, it's always better to be the first to arrive, or at least to arrive on time to show that the appointment is a priority for you.

SPEAK EASY

You spot Susie walking up the street with another friend you haven't met yet. She points to the table you're at to direct her friend and walks towards you. You make eye contact with Susie's friend, smile warmly, and then you flick your eyes to Susie as your smile brightens before waving.

If someone you already know brings along someone you don't know, always acknowledge the friend with a smile before continuing the greeting to show that you are open and accepting of them being there. You don't ever want to make someone feel like an outsider.

Once they reach the table, you give Susie a tight hug, saying, "It's so good to see you, Susie," remembering to say her name. Then as you release the hug, you gauge her friend for a second. She seems friendly and open so you gesture your arms to offer a hug. She accepts, and you hug her while introducing yourself warmly.

In this greeting, you have shown Susie that she's important to you, and you've made her friend feel welcome and comfortable. You have set the tone of the lunch to be warm, enjoyable, and inclusive. You've also opened yourself to making a new friend.

Social greetings should be warm, light-hearted, and enjoyable for everyone. You want to be open and welcoming with an essence of joy in your demeanor. Don't let yourself shy away or make less effort because it's not for a serious occasion. Make an effort with your social greetings, and you will keep old friends as well as make new ones.

Casual

It's Friday night and you're at the bar with your friends. There are people you've met before all around you and strangers too. The atmosphere is relaxed as you hold a drink in your hands. Everyone is here to unwind from a long week and have a bit of social fun.

The friend next to you heads to the restroom, and a stranger sits down in their place. They seem open and vibrant, and they're around your age. You turn to them for a second and as they turn and look in your eyes briefly, you smile kindly. They smile back and look happy to engage.

It's noisy at the bar, so you lean in, put your hand on their upper arm and introduce yourself. You remove your hand as soon as you're done talking, and they lean in to introduce themselves in return.

In this case, you want to keep any touching platonic and to a minimum but don't leave it out completely unless the person doesn't seem comfortable with it. A subtle touch will naturally communicate trust and provoke feelings of connection. You can disguise it as necessary, such as in this case, using the person's upper arm to help you lean in to talk over the noise.

Nailing a greeting in a casual setting where there are multiple people whom you haven't met can help you initiate conversations easily, make you feel confident and comfortable as you turn strangers into acquaintances, and open you up to meeting valuable people you might cherish for years to come.

Formal

It's your colleague's wedding, and you've put on your best formal wear. The ceremony is done and you're heading to the reception with your plus one. Before everyone settles down for dinner, you see your colleague's parents and decide to go over and congratulate them on their daughter's marriage.

They're standing together with a glass of champagne in their hands, overlooking the event with pride. You approach them confidently, catch each of their eyes for a moment, and smile warmly. Once you reach them you offer your right hand for a handshake as you introduce yourself and offer your sentiment.

In this case, you don't have to give such a firm handshake. Keep it moderate and confident. You can also adjust your greeting if you are greeting the opposite sex. For example, some women may prefer a gentler handshake or even a brief holding of their hand with a soft squeeze if you are male, and some men may prefer a hug over a handshake if you are a woman.

In this case, you can try to get a read on the person you're greeting before approaching them and look out for any signs or gestures indicating what they'd prefer. For example a man opening his arms to initiate a hug or a woman holding out a hand with the palm facing down. Trust your gut feeling on what is appropriate.

Intimate

You've been speaking to a romantic interest online for a couple of days and have decided to go on a date with them. You've already exchanged fondness for each other and feel excited to meet them in person. As you arrive, you see them waiting outside of the restaurant for you.

Making eye contact, your eyes glint with excitement, and you allow your smile to light up your face entirely. They're everything you expected. When you reach them, you touch their forearm, caressing it slightly, and seeing their returned enthusiasm you exchange a peck on the cheek. You say, "It's so nice to meet you in person," followed by their name.

In this instance, you've used the same four steps you would use for the most professional meeting and transformed them into a communication of romance. You've shown your date that you are excited about seeing them, you are interested in them romantically, and that you are present with them.

The four steps you've seen put into practice will set you up for making an excellent first impression. Without a lot of legwork, first impressions usually stick. So, instead of trying to scramble your reputation back together, make sure you put your best foot forward as often as possible. There is space in your Workbook to reflect on these steps and any areas in your life where you would most like to exercise them.

But your greeting is just the beginning. Your positive impression needs to be memorable rather than momentary. That's how first impressions lead to long-term likability and influence. So, meet me in the next chapter, and let me show you how to extend your incredible energy throughout every interaction you have.

13

MEMORABLE INTERACTIONS

How To Ensure Every Conversation Leaves
The Most Positive Impression

*"Human connections are deeply nurtured
in the field of a shared story."*

– Jean Houston

Walking up to the counter of my favorite local cafe, I noticed a new barista operating the coffee machine. After placing my order with her, the necklace she was wearing caught my eye. It was a symbol I recognized from Greek mythology so I decided to compliment her on it. To my surprise, she beamed with passion over the subject as she prepared my coffee.

Being a quiet day, I stood at the counter and chatted excitedly with her for a moment, feeling the spark of a new friendship emerge. We spoke like we'd known each other forever and reveled in the mutual interest in ancient symbols and mythology. Another customer walked in, so she quickly scribbled her number on my slip and said, "Let's meet up sometime?" Confirming with a nod, I read her name tag and left with a "Great to meet you, Tash!"

Now this isn't a story about another effective communicator who influenced my life. At first, Tash seemed like another rare find, a person so eager to connect that she engaged fully with every anecdote, story, or finding we shared. But, after getting to know her and embracing her as another keen friend in my life, I quickly started to pick up on some discrepancies.

Listen carefully. There's an important lesson here.

Tash is a perfect example of someone who knows how to make a great first impression without having the substance to take her well-practiced bubbly energy all the way. She's certainly not a bad person, but her intentions shine through the more you get to know her. I don't want you to be like Tash. I want your likability to last forever.

On first impression, Tash was bright-eyed and engaging, doing all the right things to communicate interest. But, the minute the topic swayed to something other than herself or her interests, her eyes glazed over, she notably sighed in boredom, and she left me feeling shut down. This was a recurring pattern. I quickly learned that when I made an effort to restrain myself from talking and allowed her to dominate the conversation, she would brighten up again. The friendship became draining.

At first I tried to remedy the situation, trying to acknowledge any part I had to play in our conflict, but soon I realized that my efforts were wasted. She seemed to go through friends like a fire through a forest, drawing you in with initial warmth before burning you down and moving to the next person. So, instead of taking it personally, I distanced myself and moved on.

What is the point of giving a great first impression if it's bound to fade? First impressions alone do not guarantee likability. Yes, they influence it greatly, but without strong communication skills, and a lasting impression, people will catch on. Your energy will give you away, whether you know it or not.

To transform your impression from momentary to memorable, you must consider three things:

- The energy you bring to the table
- The conversations you keep
- The energy you leave behind

Each aspect is as important as the next. Firstly, the energy you bring to the table refers to your first impression. This will affect your interactions for a long time, but they can and do fizzle out if you prove them wrong.

Secondly, you need to take care of the conversations you keep. You need to be able to hold and enhance them. They can't be ego-driven and self-serving. They must uplift both you and the person you're conversing with. The way you navigate conversations, both good and bad, will teach others a lot about who you are.

And lastly, the energy you leave behind is the energy that lingers with the person long after the interaction is over – let's call it your lasting impression. This is all about how you make people feel.

But let's start at the beginning.

YOUR FIRST IMPRESSION

By now, I know you've done a lot of work on your level of self-awareness. You've grown immensely since Chapter 4 and deserve recognition for that. You've also moved on to facing your insecurities with bravery. Your confidence is so much more than what it used to be. Now it's time to put what you've learned to practice in the real world. Show others what a charming, likable person you are! Your first opportunity to do that is with your first impression.

It only takes 0.1 seconds for someone to form an initial impression of you.[7] As time goes on, that impression merely solidifies and often becomes more indifferent. That means the better your first impression is, the more likely it is to remain a positive first impression. But, if you give an indifferent impression from the start, it is more likely to turn negative.

You know how to ace a greeting from start to finish, but I want to teach you how to make sure that the first 0.1 seconds are as impactful as possible. This all comes down to your energy, also known as your presence, aka your intentions, positive attitude, authenticity, and curiosity. You can't nail a greeting without it.

By now, you have actively worked on your energy and have a good understanding of how you come across to others in general. Your intentions are pure, and you *want* to make a genuinely excellent impression on everyone you meet. But what happens if you're having a bad day?

Surely your inner light is naturally going to be a little dimmer than usual sometimes. How do you make sure your first impression is as good as possible without pretending that you're fine when you're not? After all, effective communication is all about authenticity, right? How do you light up a room when you feel switched off? And how do you make sure your bad day doesn't inadvertently paint you in a bad light? Let me show you.

There are three strategies you can use if you don't feel your best but want to maintain your reputation. You are human, and having bad days is completely okay, no matter how social, magnetic, or energetic you normally are. All you have to do is adjust your approach.

You also don't have to feel obligated to socialize when you're not up for it. But, sometimes socializing is unavoidable, and you don't want to let a bad day spoil potential connections. So, use your self-awareness to gauge how open you feel before an event or social interaction, and take note when you're not at your best. Then, use these tips to confidently make the best first impression you can:

Tune Up Your Energy

It's amazing how quickly you can turn a bad day around with a little intent and effort. Even if you have major life events bringing you down, taking a bit of time to tune up your energy before going out can significantly improve your first impression. You will likely enjoy yourself far more too.

Before you head out to a social event, intentionally engage in activities that uplift you. A bad day or consistent stress depletes you, so counteract that by doing things that replenish you. Things that improve your energy can include:

- Listening to your favorite uplifting music.
- Light exercise like walking or yoga.
- Watching comedy movies, series, or stand-up.
- Engaging in a hobby you love.
- Eating a wholesome meal.
- Journaling about the problem.
- Lying down or taking a quick nap.
- Confiding in someone you trust.

Adjust your tune-up activities to suit what will counteract your mood best. If you're exhausted and stressed out, lying down for a bit and resting can help replenish your energy. If you're feeling down and overthinking, watching comedy can help take your mind off things and prime you for laughter. If you're strapped for time, listening to your favorite uplifting music on your way to the event can work wonders. Music is very powerful. Don't underestimate how quickly an uplifting song can bring you back to baseline.

Use your growing sense of self-awareness to figure out your needs and do your best to meet them in some way before attempting to socialize. A little bit of effort will go a long way to shine up your first impression. Remember, the first 0.1 seconds counts the most, so build up your energy as much as you can beforehand.

Focus On Them

Sometimes, a distraction is enough to completely take your mind off of what's bringing you down. Instead of worrying about what you're going to say or how you're going to present yourself, transfer your focus onto the other person. Doing this activates your curiosity, gives you a chance to practice heart-led listening, and makes you more likable, even when you feel bad.

People love to talk about themselves or their interests. When you don't have the energy to bring much to the table, why not hand the spotlight over to somebody else? Focus on asking great questions and using the time to find out more about them. Allow your mind to center on the moment and forget about whatever's been bothering you.

Be Vulnerable

It's far better to leave a first impression as someone who was having a bad day than someone ingenuine. Don't be afraid to express vulnerability. If something's wrong, people will feel it one way or another. Rather be straightforward about it than wait for people to notice something is off and potentially misinterpret you.

You don't have to open up a monologue about your problems. Just give a casual confirmation that you're not having a great day to avoid seeming fake. Use your bad day as an opportunity to showcase how you cope with problems. Rather than letting your stress reveal a bad attitude, let it reveal how brave you are in the face of adversity. How well you deal with stress, conflict, and sickness is a reflection of your character. Be genuine and you're far more likely to make a good first impression.

THE CONVERSATIONS YOU KEEP

First impressions set the tone for the rest of any conversation you have and often affect the connections you build moving forward, too. But they aren't everything. To communicate effectively, you need to go above and beyond what most people are willing to do. You have to maintain your good energy throughout entire interactions, holding conversations with care and enhancing them.

People with effective communication skills help steer conversations in a more positive direction, and they make sure everyone involved enjoys themselves. You don't have to be hypervigilant to each person, but you do have to be considerate. However, everyone matters, including you.

Your conversations should never be ego-driven or self-serving, but you do need to feel fulfilled by them as much as everyone else. It needs to be a comfortable give and take of great energy. Remember, you're not here to become a people pleaser. You want to uplift people and have a memorable interaction, but never at your expense. Memorable conversations are exciting, balanced, and enjoyable for *everyone*.

The conversations you keep are a reflection of who you are. If your main focus is to get something out of it, like how Tash only seemed interested when she could gain something, it shows that you are self-serving. However, if your focus is to be liked no matter what, it shows that you have unresolved insecurities. The same goes for your ability to deal with conflict, but we'll speak more on that in the next chapter.

I want your conversations to reflect your graciousness, confidence, and grit. You should enhance every conversation you enter without throwing your needs to the side. You're here to become well-liked for who you are and successful. So show people what you've got, and let your conversational skills do the talking.

Leading great interactions is going to take every trait of effective communication you've learned. This is how you can apply them:

Self-awareness

You know yourself best. Make sure you move forward in any conversation presenting yourself as the person you want to be. Stay aware of how others react to you, and make sure to adjust your level of intensity to match or uplift the conversation. If you notice yourself acting in a way that you're trying to avoid, remind yourself that you've made an effort to improve, and you deserve to maintain your new reputation.

Observe your behavior in conversation and notice the reactions you get. Then, adjust your behavior to match the person you want to be rather than who you've always been. You're not going to get a different result by behaving the same way you always have, so be willing to change and actively improve your behavior.

Empathy

Use your empathy to understand how the people you're with are feeling. Then adjust your behavior and words to accommodate them. Remember, empathy involves understanding how someone else feels, validating their feelings by differentiating their feelings from yours, and showing them that you understand and care. It goes a long way in creating memorable conversations with everyone you meet.

The more heard and validated someone feels in your presence, the more open they will be around you. Authentic and vulnerable conversations often make for the most memorable interactions.

Non-verbal Communication

To adjust your behavior means to make sure you communicate your intentions accurately. Remember, your nonverbal cues make up the majority of your communications, so make sure they are saying what you want them to say.

Stay aware of your reactions and movements, such as body posture, gestures, and facial expressions. Take a moment now and then to recognize and adjust your tone of voice if needed. Use touch and haptics to communicate your level of closeness and connection with the person.

Make sure you are being as authentic as possible to avoid giving off the feeling that you aren't genuine. Self-awareness is your greatest ally to having the presence you want to have.

A Positive Attitude

It's easier to communicate the emotions we want when our inner world and attitude are balanced. People with effective communication skills have an optimistic mindset, allowing them to see opportunities where others see lack. Be sure to express your positive attitude unapologetically during conversation. Unless someone is deeply pessimistic, positivity is often a refreshing and welcomed trait to witness.

Use your positive attitude to remind yourself why you're here. Genuine connection is the most valuable resource on earth, but you won't achieve it if you don't believe in it.

Heart-led Listening

It's not enough to be a good listener in conversation, you need to be a heart-led listener first. That means letting your heart guide your listening and not the biases, doubts, and false beliefs of your mind. You need to listen with true, authentic empathy. That means listening with good intentions rather than selfish ones.

Pair excellent listening skills with a genuine desire to understand and care for memorable interactions that'll impact people for a lifetime.

Curiosity, Intelligence, And Authenticity

Your presence needs to bring out the best in the people around you. Tap into your child-like curiosity and enter conversations with a deep desire to listen, observe, and learn. Let your passion shine through wildly as you speak, then with the right questions and level of intrigue draw out the passion of those around you.

Confidence

Confidence is not arrogance. Entering conversations with confidence means staying silent if you have to. Be the rock in a sea of chaos so that those who stop to join in conversation with you are anchored in by your presence.

The more at ease you are within yourself, the more stable and attractive you will be. Know your worth, love yourself, and trust that you can handle whatever turn a conversation takes with grace and skill. Let your confidence be something you exude, not something you expel.

Humor

Whether you're in a good or bad mood, you should always prime yourself for laughter before being around people. It's easy to forget to see the humor in life. Take time to exercise your sense of humor as often as you can. The more fun, silly, and hilarious you can be when it's appropriate, the easier it will be to remember you. The bursts of laughter, moments of absurdity, and hilarious mix-ups are often the moments you talk about for years after an event. Make sure you're a part of the lighter side of any conversation.

YOUR LASTING IMPRESSION

You're here to be exceptional. You're here to be memorable. And you're here because you want to build authentic, long-lasting connections with people. A first impression and effective communication skills are not going to cut it. You need to go above and beyond what most people are willing to do.

To enjoy the most memorable interactions with someone, you must make a lasting emotional impression on them. Much like a first impression is the way someone interprets how you feel and who you are, your lasting impression is how you leave someone feeling.

We often remember moments by emotions, and that's why we remember people by the way they make us feel rather than what they say or do. To leave a lasting impression that will have people recalling their incredible time with you, you need to:

- Grab their attention
- Find mutual ground
- Become a great storyteller
- Say how you feel
- Make an effort to say goodbye

Remember, people with effective communication skills are so excellent because they do what other people aren't willing to. If you want to be memorable, you absolutely need to do the same. Here's how:

Grab Their Attention

What happens when you hear your name called out above a crowd? It won't matter what you're doing or who you're talking to, it's going to grab your attention. In the same way, taking opportunities to say someone's name in conversation brings their focus onto you. Without even realizing it, they will find themselves listening more intently and thinking more highly of you.

When you're in conversation with anyone, whether it's someone you've known a long time or someone you've just met, I want you to find ways to say their name more often. This can sound like:

"Hey, James, what do you think of this?"

"Amy, I love that story!"

"You know, Michael, what you said has me thinking."

More often than not, we tend to underdo it but do be careful not to overdo it. Pay attention to the flow of conversation and get comfortable using names to grip the focus back onto you and show the person you respect and acknowledge them.

Names are a label people identify with deeply. It's a label for their identity. If you make an effort to remember someone's name and use it in conversation, it can send the message that you see them and accept them. It's an easy way to harbor instant attraction and rapport.

Find Mutual Ground

The quickest way to keep a conversation flowing is to look out for topics of mutual interest and roll with them. Don't be afraid to fish around the conversation, bringing up different topics or asking questions. The sooner you can find mutual ground to stand on, the sooner you'll find connection, interest, and excitement together.

Don't make the mistake of diving straight into topics you're interested in without making sure the other person is as well. Read the person to look out for genuine interest. If they're feigning interest to make you happy, you might enjoy the conversation while they're secretly waiting for it to be over. Never let that happen. There are two ways to be memorable, for the right reasons and the wrong reasons. Make sure you're memorable for the right reasons.

That doesn't mean you can never talk about your interests unless they're mutual, only that you need to be aware of the other person's experience. If they are genuinely interested or curious about what you have to say, go for it. But if you get a sense of awkwardness or see the person losing interest, change topics.

Become A Great Storyteller

To be memorable, you need to play an active role in conversation. Listening is incredibly important, but it shouldn't leave you on the sidelines. If you are practicing heart-led listening that improves the flow of conversation, you will still have plenty of time to talk. Make it count.

When you are in the spotlight, telling a story or making a point, don't let it fall flat. Your energy must translate through your words and make the conversation more vibrant. You need to become a great storyteller. Pull your listeners into the very moment you are speaking of and make even the simplest story memorable and moving. Do that, and people will hang on every word you say. Here's how:

- **Step 1 - Believe in your story:** Believing in your story will give you the confidence to sell it and grab people's attention. Your confidence will translate through your body language.

- **Step 2 - Get clear about the direction:** Eliminate the chances of getting lost in your own story by making sure you're clear about the direction. Hook your company in with a sneak peek of the outcome and then work your way to it from the beginning.

- **Step 3 - Stay on topic:** Don't branch out unless it's going to add value, humor, or intrigue to your story. If you're losing the point, so will your audience.

- **Step 4 - Open up:** Add elements of vulnerability. If you felt a certain way or did something you're not proud of to get to the end result, open up! Remember, vulnerability creates relatability, and relatability creates connection.

- **Step 5 - Follow through:** Carry the energy you had at the beginning of your story all the way through to the end.

> If your energy fades towards the end of your story, the punchline won't land, and people will lose interest. Get out of your own head, don't worry about the opinions of others, and finish your story with enthusiasm.

A great storyteller captivates their audience. Whenever you tell a story, capture as much emotion and detail as you can, then bring it home. Great storytellers stay memorable and relevant long after the conversation is over. I want that for you, so make the effort and watch it pay off.

Say How You Feel

Vulnerability is not always about opening up about negative things like our struggles or failures. Sometimes, the best and most memorable vulnerability is positive vulnerability. This is when you open up about the positive emotions or thoughts you're having.

If you feel positive about someone, be upfront about it. Tell people when you find them interesting, funny, likable, or beautiful. Chances are, they haven't heard these things very often. We tend to be secretive about how we feel, only going as far as to show someone that we care in the ways we know. But there is power in *saying* how we feel. Words stick in the mind.

Instead of being passive when building relationships, take the chances that you get to vocalize your positive thoughts and feelings. Not only will your words leave people thinking about you long after the interaction is over, but they will ensure the impression you make is positive.

Being upfront about your positive thoughts and feelings shows how little you fear rejection. It shows that you are sure of yourself, which makes others sure about you.

Make An Effort To Say Goodbye

It's too easy to quickly slip away from a busy social gathering. But your final moments with someone can make or break your lasting impression. A little effort goes a long way, and that is still true for the effort you put into saying goodbye to someone.

You don't need to overcomplicate things. Simply make the effort to express your gratitude for the time spent together and part ways with warmth. A great goodbye is the cherry on top of your lasting impression. It shows people you value them and brings your interaction to a memorable close.

Of course, it's easier if you are already speaking to someone when you decide to leave. But, when you've made wonderful connections across a crowded room, try to approach each person one final time if possible. Keep it simple. Use what you've learned to convey the emotion you want to convey. Say something genuine about your interaction with them, use touch to show that you care, and leave with a smile.

Now that we've covered the 3 areas to leave a memorable impression, reflect on any thoughts you have in your Workbook. Consider which area you could work on the most and how to implement positive changes in your daily interactions. Come back when you're done to finish this chapter and move on to the next.

SPEAK EASY

Like an Olympian who makes swimming look as easy as breathing, effective communication is about making your glowing personality look effortless. You know it takes work to be kind, caring, and confident, but to those around you, you simply emanate charisma. However, like the Olympian, with time, dedication, and practice, your hard work will pay off, and what used to feel like effort becomes emanation nonetheless. This is when you become socially aware, tactfully brilliant, and magnetic to the core. So, turn the page again, and be prepared to learn how to let your charisma shine through in any given social situation, from seamless networking to courage and kindness in conflict.

Note: This marks the end of Day 6. There's only one day left to go! Soak up today's knowledge and get some rest before starting Day 7, the final step on your 7-day journey.

14

SOCIALLY AWARE & TACTFULLY BRILLIANT

Applying Your Effective Communication Skills In Real Time

"Communication - the human connection - is the key to personal and career success"

– Paul J. Meyer

Right now, your foundation of effective communication is becoming cemented. It's reaching down, gripping the fabric of your identity, and it's about to change your life forever. Remember the chocolate wrapper analogy from Chapter 3? Well, it works in reverse as well.

You've been going through a transformation. You've adopted and practiced effective communication skills. But it's one thing to feel like a ray of sunshine within yourself and another for the world to interpret your new energy correctly and change its perception of you.

For your new identity to become who you are, you must become comfortable with effective communication from the inside out. Don't keep it an internal experience that only you're aware of. Allow it to seep through in every moment. Let it polish up your interactions and gain you the success and happiness you crave.

It's time to put what you've learned into solid practice and show the world who you are. Use your effective communication skills to ace every job interview you enter. Don't be shy. Let them enhance your words as you give an important speech. Tailor them to help you sway conflict in a positive direction. Use them. You've learned what you must; now make it work for you. Take what you learn in this chapter and apply it to all areas of your life.

NETWORKING

The relationships you build in a professional setting are often the conveyor belt moving your career forward. Let them deteriorate, and everything comes to a halt. Nourish them, and your career flourishes. That's where networking comes in.

But networking has a bad reputation for being difficult and opportunistically driven. Even though there are several statistics to prove how beneficial networking is for job success, you need to approach it differently. Don't think about all you can gain from the people you meet, but rather what you can offer. That kind of genuine approach will work out far better in the long term.

To use networking effectively, you should absolutely:

- Tune up your energy and make a memorable impression.
- Focus on making loyal, mutually valuable connections.
- Bring all that you can offer to the table first before making any requests.
- Lean toward more intimate conversations instead of small talk.
- Ask intriguing questions, then practice heart-led listening.

Don't let the potential gains of networking get to your head. Stay authentic and humble while you use your communication skills to impact everyone you meet. Ensure your attitude is in check and your intentions are pure so your skills can make the most positive impact possible.

JOB INTERVIEWS

Memorability is key for job interviews. You need to stand out, make a solid impression, and walk away having overshadowed your resume with your energy and impact. There are plenty of tips available for acing job interviews, including being prepared, being on time, and taking notes. But you can use your communication skills to give you a significant edge in any interview. People who communicate effectively are the most memorable because they:

- Naturally show up with a positive demeanor and enthusiasm.
- Give a confident and warm greeting with a smile.
- Hold confident and comfortable body language.
- Communicate clearly and concisely.
- Are always honest and genuine.
- Focus on what value they can offer rather than gain.
- Show gratitude for the interviewer's time.

Use your effective communication skills to read the energy of the interview and put your best foot forward. Be professional, but don't be afraid to show your personality and passion.

PUBLIC SPEAKING

Your effective communication skills don't only help you succeed in one-on-one conversations. They can drastically improve your stage presence, too. Your confident body language, smooth hand gestures, and vibrant tone will grab the audience's attention and make the stage your own. These are the fundamentals of successful public speaking:

- Knowing the audience
- Preparation and practice

- A professional appearance
- Great non-verbal communication
- Clear and well-paced delivery
- Audience retention and engagement
- Management of nerves
- A strong call to action

Go to your Workbook now and see this list written out with a space below each point. Write down next to each one how effective communication can help improve it. You've got a great understanding of what it means to communicate effectively; now put it to the test. See if you can identify ways to use your skills for public speaking. When you're done, read on and compare your answers.

How to use effective communication skills to help you ace the fundamentals of public speaking:

- **Knowing the audience:** Do your research and tailor your speech to meet the audience's needs rather than your own. Consider what they hope to gain from the speech and deliver it.

- **Preparation and practice:** With a positive attitude, put in the work before your speech by practicing in front of the mirror or a trusted person. Be kind to yourself, and encourage yourself to be confident about the outcome. Don't doubt yourself. Get excited! There is no better time to use the "tune up your energy" approach than before a speech.

- **A professional appearance:** Have pride in your appearance and make sure you dress the part. Looking your best comes with making a memorable impression.

- **Great non-verbal communication:** Effective communication includes exceptional control and awareness of your non-verbal cues. Hold a confident posture, smile warmly, and speak with integrity. And don't forget about eye contact! Take time during your speech to look people in the eyes one at a time to convey trust and engage.

- **Clear and well-paced delivery:** Communicate with confidence. Use a smooth pace that is slower than you expect, avoid filler words, and get comfortable with silent pauses.

- **Audience retention and engagement:** Consider the audience and ask open-ended questions to get them thinking. Include them, show them interesting pictures or videos, and use your storytelling skills to keep them hooked. Sprinkle in a touch of humor and allow the audience time to react.

- **Management of nerves:** It's normal to experience nerves during a speech. The pressure is on to do your best and all eyes are on you. Do what you can to keep your nerves down. Shift your focus onto the outcome of your speech and breathe. Pause, reflect, and keep going.

- **A strong call to action:** Ending your speech with a powerful call to action or hard-hitting, open-ended question is a great way to leave a lasting impression on your audience. Imagine what emotion you want to leave the audience with, and make it happen. Leave them thinking, feeling, and remembering your speech long after it's over.

Your public speaking appearances can impact your reputation greatly. Although daunting, the only thing standing in your way is yourself. It takes confidence, empathy, and excellent execution to give a great speech. But you have the tools. Use them.

CONFLICTUAL DISCUSSIONS

Effective communication takes persistence. It's not about putting on a front that suddenly strips away the minute you face conflict. It's about showing up authentically, empathetically, and confidently in any situation. To handle conflict gracefully:

- Start with empathy and listen.
- Take responsibility for your mistakes and flaws.
- Be open and honest about how you feel.
- Practice self-love and express your boundaries.
- Have confidence and be forthright.
- Use your self-awareness to keep calm.
- Focus on finding solutions.
- Move on quickly once the conflict is resolved.
- Learn and grow from it.

Conflict is not about winning. It is about being amicable. The focus must always be on finding a solution that both parties can agree on. Listen to the other person and try to understand their point of view. Don't hold grudges. Learn to move on in peace and leave conflict in the past once you've worked through it. The quicker you can resolve a conflict in a kind and straightforward way, the less likely it is to damage your relationships.

Relationships are valuable. Don't let something as inevitable as conflict spoil something otherwise healthy. Take the lesson from it all and shift your focus to something more positive as soon as possible. And, if possible, try to see the humor in it. Conflictual discussions can get heated, and high emotions can make us act silly. Laugh at yourself, conflict doesn't always have to be so serious.

CUSTOMER SERVICE

Connected people have empathy. They look people in the eye and acknowledge them with kindness and understanding. Whether you're a customer service worker or a customer, effective communication skills go a long way to improve the mundane moments of everyday life in society.

The last time you ordered coffee at a restaurant, who served you? Do you remember what they looked like, and did you bother to greet them? Did they smile before walking away, or did they leave looking bored or stressed by the interaction? The impact you make on service workers matters. But this time, it's not about your reputation, it's about your sense of humanity. Connected people care about how they make people feel – all people. You should, too.

Use your energy to make the world a better place. Everybody deserves to be acknowledged during an interaction with you. Make an effort to improve even the most mundane moments and feel how your life uplifts. Smile and look your waitress in the eyes. Ask her how she's doing before simply jabbering your order to her. Say thank you when she leaves and watch her face light up as she feels seen and appreciated.

Take notice of how you make service workers feel. Read them after they've interacted with you, and use your self-awareness to understand the changes you see in them. However, if *you're* a service worker, you are responsible for your half of the interaction. Your energy can influence your experience with customers greatly.

There are many overlapping traits between a highly successful customer service employee and someone with effective communication skills. To excel in a customer service career, you need to have patience and be able to adapt to each customer, two things that require an acute level of empathy. But you also need to have a warm presence and a positive attitude.

I won't deny that service workers aren't always treated well by customers, which often causes them to lose their enthusiasm for the job. But your effort can turn things around overnight.

Think about it. What makes working with people awful? Once you have a list of negative experiences to refer to, it's easier to anticipate more negative interactions. Each time this anticipation is confirmed by another negative experience with a customer, a negative narrative about your job follows. Effective communication can help you break free from that and enjoy your job again. The key to overcoming disillusionment with your career is curiosity.

Instead of approaching your customers with anticipation, approach them with an open mind. Give people the benefit of the doubt and observe their behavior. As a customer service worker, you're likely trained to approach customers with a positive attitude. Do what you can to tune up your energy before going to work. Honor your needs as best you can and remind yourself why being open and connected is important to you. With your communication skills at the forefront, you'll not only succeed in your job, but you'll find your passion for it again.

TEAMWORK AND COLLABORATION

Effective communicators are the ultimate team players because they are great leaders with high emotional intelligence. When working with others in a collaborative setting, you have to be able to lead with confidence, manage your emotions, and also make space for others to lead as well.

Teamwork is not about one person calling the shots; it's a collaborative effort to reach a mutual goal. You often need to rely on each other's unique skill sets to get the job done. You can't let yourself take over, and you can't shrink into the background. You must show up with enthusiasm and willingness to work within the team. Great teamwork takes:

- Effective communication skills
- Leadership ability
- Problem solving
- Active listening

- Emotional intelligence
- Conflict management
- Motivation and passion

Use the traits you've learned, and don't be afraid to lead. Even though successful collaboration means equal effort and interest, you can find ways to encourage others with your positive attitude, leadership, and determination. Lead in the role you play within a team, and it will inspire others to do the same.

SOCIAL MEDIA

Most people with a phone have some form of social media, and it's become a popular tool for connecting both socially and professionally. That's why your social media presence matters. It greatly impacts the way the world perceives you. If you want your true character to permeate, don't forget about the content you post – down to your profile pictures and comments.

A lot goes into a magnetic social media presence, but the goal should always be the same. Your social media should represent who you are in an authentic way. The effective approach to your online presence is all about being YOU. It's not about trying to be someone you're not. The more real you are online, the better people will feel when meeting you in person. They will feel like they already know you to some degree, and they won't feel disappointed when they find out you're exactly who you say you are.

It's also important to remember that although social media is about building connections and making a positive impact, it's not that serious. You can have fun with it! And you should. Use it to reveal your sense of humor and your hobbies. Be a little bit vulnerable. Be raw, be real. You're multifaceted. Let your social media show the many sides of you, not just the carefully chosen ones.

In this modern world, the way we connect to each other has evolved. It's not all about in-person interaction anymore. We can now make connections all over the world with just a click of a button. Be aware of that, grateful for it, and don't underestimate it.

But whichever ways you choose to connect with people, one thing is certain: human connections are extremely valuable to us. If you think about it, they are the most valuable human resource on earth. That's why you're here, aren't you? You've come to enhance your personality so that you can magnetize people into your life that make it better.

People are the source of our greatest joys and pains. People help create success for us, but they can also take it away. They bring love, heartbreak, lessons, friendship, and valuable insights. We learn from each other more than anything else in the world. And there is so much power in that if you recognize it. That's why I need you to turn the page right now and come with me on the final but most valuable benefit of effective communication – building strong, mutually beneficial relationships that last a lifetime and change you for the better.

15

BUILDING STRONG RELATIONSHIPS

How To Apply Effective Communication Skills To Various Professional And Personal Relationships

"But the law of magnetism really is true: who you are is who you attract."

– John C Maxwell

In Part One, you got a feeling for the wonderful impact a magnetic, connected person can have on your life. They can make you feel included, important, and excited to be your authentic self. Their warmth is addictive, it's infectious. This is the role you play now. YOU draw people in with your smile and confidence. YOU light up the rooms you enter, promising a positive impact on the people there. And it's YOU who makes people feel comfortable and excited to be themselves.

Your impact is powerful and it's important that you carry that power with care and good intentions. And don't worry, as much as you've learned to uplift the spaces you fill, there's something in this for you too.

Your relationships can govern how happy and successful you are. In fact, the health of your relationships is so important that your life may depend on them. According to one study, which involved over 300,000 people, a lack of meaningful connection increases your risk of premature death from all causes by 50%.[8] We're social beings that can't survive without strong relationships, let alone feel fulfilled without them. But there's a catch.

Relationships can make our lives blissful, or they can make them a living hell. Which way the pendulum swings is up to you. Relationships are a two-way street, and you have a greater role to play than you realize. You decide if your relationships help you or hinder you.

Effective communication makes the choice easy.

It's adaptable. It's something that you can shape to improve any relationship. It comes with skills that give you the interpersonal edge you need to be well-liked and respected no matter who you are, how old you are, or where your reputation currently stands. It can help you become a chameleon, adjusting yourself with empathy and honesty so you can get along with anyone.

Being adaptable in relationships is not about being fake, wearing a mask, or changing who you are. It's simply about subtly shapeshifting your approach to succeed and connect. Everyone is different and can only meet you where they are. So, instead of letting important relationships dissolve or recoil, you can use effective communication to build powerful connections around differences or flaws.

All it takes is understanding kindness, and a willingness to love people unconditionally. You can choose to see the good in people instead of focusing on their shortcomings. You don't have to keep relationships that are abusive or one-sided, but you can use your effective communication skills to navigate otherwise good relationships with ease.

Remember, effective communication is outward-focused. But that doesn't mean you won't get anything out of it. Building strong relationships offers many benefits, including:

- A support system you can rely on when life gets tough.
- Valuable resources of wisdom and experience you can tap into.
- A space where you're understood and loved.
- Better health and well-being both mentally and physically.

- A sense of purpose that fulfills you.

These benefits are not limited to romantic relationships. They can come from any strong relationship you make the effort to build. But different relationships have different challenges. That's where your adaptability comes in.

Some relationships call for a lot of joy, silliness, and love. But others require a level of respect and seriousness that makes them work as they should. Your ability to gauge and adapt to various relationships is going to determine how your life turns out. In this chapter – the final chapter – I'm going to give you a useful breakdown of how effective communication can improve and deepen any relationship you have. I'm going to show you how it can shift the balance of your life from going nowhere to somewhere great through the power of human connection alone. Are you ready?

PROFESSIONAL

One sour relationship can plunge you into a world of cortisol. When your body is fueled by stress and anxiety you're bound to make poor choices and ultimately mistakes. That's one thing when it's someone from your personal life, but when it's someone in your professional life the impact can be tremendous.

Your success relies on the professional relationships you keep, from your supervisor down to your coworkers and clients. Whatever business or industry you're in, even if you work from home, effective communication can help keep your slate clean. Don't ever be the one causing unnecessary conflict. Use your skills to stay professional, warm, and positive in everyone's eyes. To help you successfully navigate the important professional relationships you're in, let me break them down:

Supervisors

There are ways to handle both sides of any relationship appropriately. The supervisor and employee relationship is often tough, especially when employees are unhappy in their career choices or when supervisors feel the need to be cold-hearted. Whichever side of the coin you're on, effective communication can solve these problems.

If you're a supervisor, there is likely a lot of pressure on your shoulders. You are responsible for your own duties *and* foreseeing the duties of multiple other employees. If your employees are indifferent to their jobs, it's easy to feel frustrated and confrontational. However, you're here to learn a new approach to life, so take notes.

Instead of staying closed off from the employees under your watch, open up to them. Don't jump to conclusions about their experience or use force to get them to complete tasks, listen to them and encourage them. Think of your role as a leadership position. Lead by example and inspire the employees to care about their work.

And if you're struggling to shake your frustration, consider where your attitude is regarding your career. If your mind is filled with negative thoughts and anticipation, work on yourself before letting it out on employees. Tune up your energy before dealing with anyone else, and try to enter a confrontation with empathy and an open mind. The more open and respectful you are with employees, the more likely they are to trust you, confide in you, and show you respect in return.

However, if you are an employee with a supervisor hanging over your shoulders, it is important that you find a way to show them respect. Show up at work in the best headspace you possibly can and make an effort to do a great job. If your supervisor is tough, become curious about why. Try to understand that they are responsible for you and are likely under a lot of pressure.

If you're struggling to show up at work with a positive attitude, make an effort to practice gratitude for your job. Every profession comes with challenges; do your best to tackle them with dignity and grace. And if you can't change something, focus on the positive aspects of your work. I know it's easier said than done, but make sure you don't sabotage a great position because you overlooked the positives.

A bad relationship with your supervisor can result in more frequent mistakes at work and an unpleasant day-to-day experience. Shift your approach and do what you can to show them respect. Arriving at work with a can-do attitude and an inclination for respect will bring out the best in your supervisor, improving life for you both.

Coworkers

Coworker relationships can be some of the most impactful for job success and satisfaction as you likely interact with them the most during work hours. Great coworker relationships can make your day-to-day work experience a blast as you confide in each other, support each other, and find joy together throughout the day. Poor coworker relationships can add significant stress to your work, leaving you feeling isolated and distracted. Make sure your coworker relationships are healthy.

You and your coworkers are a team. If you're clashing, it's only going to hinder the success of everyone. But your attitude can help smooth things over. Use your relationships with coworkers to inspire their best efforts. Lead by example, offer support, and exercise your teamwork abilities. If you can help inspire everyone to pull their weight, your work life will improve significantly. I'm not saying it's your responsibility to mollycoddle everyone, but your energy at work has an impact on coworkers.

Make an effort to lend a listening ear when appropriate, smile and greet each of them every day, respect their boundaries, and offer your help and support when you can. Your incredible energy can brighten the atmosphere, uplift others, and encourage them to be their best too.

Customers And Clients

As someone working with clients and customers, it's your responsibility to make sure they are happy. That means tuning up your energy before talking to them and giving them the best of you. This is the time to put yourself aside fully and ground yourself in the present moment. There will be time to unwind later. They trust your authority, and they expect you to maintain a professional and helpful demeanor. Use your body language to convey relaxation and confidence, then use a friendly yet calm tone to communicate.

The more consistent you are with your professional attitude, the easier it will be to tap into that side of yourself for work and enjoy being in that headspace. As you interact with returning customers and clients, you will build a strong reputation as someone who is reliable. These relationships can improve the success of your entire company. So stick to a completely professional version of yourself and use it to approach your job with pride.

You don't have to act like a robot. But do make an effort to keep your energy positive when you are around clients. Filter out whatever is going on in your life, and keep those details for people closer to you. There is a time and a place for your personal life, and dealing with clients and customers is not one of them. If you know a client well, there's nothing wrong with being a little bit vulnerable, but for the most part, stick to your boundaries.

It's also inevitable to experience people hellbent on being unhappy in your profession. But rather than letting someone else's bad behavior encourage bad behavior in you, I want you to put yourself in their shoes to help you handle it exceptionally well. Connected people are emotionally intelligent. Don't underestimate the power your effective communication skills have to persuade and calm those around you.

Dig into your empathy to realize that there's something bigger going on for this client. And even if they seem irrational or rude, you deserve better than to stoop down to their level. Remember who you are and keep your cool. Maintain your friendly yet calm tone to avoid escalating the situation, and listen as well as you can to the client's problem. Then move on quickly, and don't let one bad experience change your demeanor toward other clients.

Patients

If you are someone who is dealing with patients, you're likely in a profession that works with people who are not at their best. Maybe you're a physiotherapist whose clients come to you in pain. Maybe you're a doctor who sees people in poor health. Or you could be a counselor who talks to people in a stressed or depressed mental state. You have a big responsibility on your shoulders. Your presence needs to be the strongest.

There's nothing better than seeing a healthcare professional who makes you feel instantly relaxed the minute you speak to them. You feel like you're in good hands and that they're going to be able to help you. The relief is instant and reassuring. But there's a good reason why they have this effect. They instill your trust in them with their great presence and care.

When you see a healthcare professional, you're likely already clued up about their level of expertise. But when you walk through the door and meet them for the first time, it's their presence and energy that confirms it. They're sure of themselves, caring, and optimistic. They welcome you with a comforting smile that says, "You're here now, let's figure this out." They put your mind at ease with their tone of voice and they make sure you leave with a calming sense of hope.

Use your effective communication skills to become a healthcare professional that has this impact on patients. Use it to emit warmth, comfort, and hope. You're likely in your profession because you're passionate about helping people. Let that passion show. You and every patient under your care will notice the difference.

Students

The student-teacher relationship is another often symbiotic relationship that can impact one another, much like the supervisor-employee relationship. If teachers are boring, harsh, or unresponsive, students switch off and lose enthusiasm. But if students don't put effort into their studies, disrupt classes, and don't show up, teachers can lose enthusiasm, too.

If you are a teacher, know that your profession is one of the most important roles in our society. You work with a part of the population who determine the future of our race. No matter what age range you teach, you are a role model to your students and your impact has the potential to change someone's outlook on life.

Your impact can lead someone down a path of passion, self-respect, and excitement. It can help someone find meaning and purpose. Let your classes teach your students more than the subject at hand. Let them learn what genuine care and guidance looks like.

As a teacher, it's up to you to inspire your students. Invoke passion within them about the subject you're teaching. Engage with them. Include them in your lessons. Let your energy show your enthusiasm and passion for the subject, as well as your desire to rope them into it. Show up to your lessons well-prepared. View your students as an audience and use what you learned about public speaking to help get your students absorbed. Try to:

- Hold a strong open posture.

- Show up prepared and in good spirits.

- Move around if you can and demonstrate.

- Greet your class warmly and smile.

- Make eye contact with them and ask them questions.

- Be confident and remember why you're there.

On the other hand, if you are a student, don't let the energy of the other students negatively influence you. Influence them. Use your keen sense of curiosity to squeeze as much out of your lessons and teachers as you can. Be a sponge. Engage with your teacher's questions and ask questions of your own. Remember that you're there to learn. Don't waste your own time, or anybody else's, by showing up bored. Try to gain as much from your learning experience as you can. Show the other students that it's respectable to engage, and break the ice to encourage them to do the same.

PERSONAL

Like we discussed in Chapter 14, success is truly about waking up every day feeling good about your life. While trouble at work can bring you down, your home space and personal life is there to bring you comfort. The relationships you build and maintain here are paramount. This is where your emotional happiness comes to rest and repair. It's where you have fun, open up, and be 100% yourself.

Personal relationships take a lot more work than professional ones. They don't have as many filters, they often involve more conflict, and they can hurt or fulfill us much more deeply. Use your effective communication skills to be a better friend, partner, parent, or sibling, and let your heart expand. These are the relationships that can turn your health around and make your life blissful. Nourish them and you will be nourished.

Family

Whether you have a functional family right now or not, pay attention here. Family doesn't always pertain to blood relatives. It can include the people in your life that you consider and treat as family. It's about the people who fill the role of a family for you. It can simply include you, your spouse, and your kids if they are all you have. Or it can include friends or distant relatives that you consider family. Whatever your family looks like, your glow, your connectedness, can significantly impact each and every one of them. It can bring your family closer and reveal the beauty and fun in each of them.

Family is all about compromise. It's about loving someone through the highs and lows of life while offering and receiving support. It's about being able to see the bigger picture behind differences and flaws, choosing to work on problems, and grow together. It's about realizing that conflict is only momentary and that your connections are more important than winning. It's knowing that anything can happen in the blink of an eye and choosing to cherish every moment instead of fixating on challenges.

It takes a lot to maintain healthy family relationships, but you have everything you need. You can be the positive anchor, setting the example of what it means to be a part of a family.

You need to be present with them, curious about their thoughts and ideas, taking the time to listen intently. You need to exercise your teamwork abilities, able to lead and be led with kindness and confidence. You must show interest in who they are and what they're about without judgment. Be your authentic self around family, opening up with vulnerability and communicating clearly to show that you trust and value them. Encourage them to do the same. Create the space for it with your warm and loving presence.

It's easy to take things personally when it comes from a family member. Practice empathy and know that their behavior is not always about you. Put yourself in their shoes and listen with the intention to understand. However, know that if you have unhealthy family relationships that you have no control over resolving, you can apply this information to the family members you already connect with instead.

Friendships

As a connected person you want to make friends wherever you go. You want to build relationships, have fun with people, and feel the loving support that friendship brings. A great friendship brings out your loyalty, your honesty, and your joy. But without the right approach, unhealthy relationships can often be disguised as friendships. That's why I must remind you that you're here to attract true connection, not people please, and camouflage your way into a bigger social circle that isn't serving you.

To attract lasting friendships, focus on your energy first. Get comfortable being yourself around potential friends and pay attention to the way that you feel. The people that are right for you will enjoy your company without needing you to change or adjust yourself for them. Your friendships should be mutually enjoyable and supportive. When you communicate effectively it's easy for people to like you and want to be your friend, but that doesn't mean they're right for you.

To avoid people who are only in your life to gain and not give, don't be afraid to be selective with your time. You can still radiate warmth and uplift people without forming a friendship. Be yourself, meet people, and enjoy the company. Then carefully decide which connections you want to frequent and deepen. You will know which relationships are worth it by the way that you feel after you're with them. If you feel drained, be weary. But if you feel energized, calmed, or inspired, listen.

Once you have formed a friendship, maintaining it is as simple as treating them with kindness and respect. Then make an effort to listen, share, and open up – vulnerability deepens relationships quickly. Make time for talking, fun, and a lot of laughter. Friendship is one of the most valuable resources for a happy life, lean into it.

Romantic

A romantic connection is a powerful relationship that can deeply change you. The kind of shift that can happen within you, whether the relationship is good or coming to an end, is powerful. Romantic connections often mirror us, revealing what is unresolved in us. If the other person is compatible with you, and you both have the skills to face differences, you can grow and transform within the relationship.

Whether you're facing relationship problems or you're happy as a clam, proper communication will only improve things. As I shared with you in Chapter 6, something as simple as using the wrong tone can escalate problems in an otherwise healthy romantic relationship. Use your self-awareness to notice where you might be going wrong, or where you can improve. Then, practice little shifts in your communication style to see the impact they have. Examples include:

- Softening your voice when speaking to your partner.
- Relaxing your body and opening your posture.
- Speaking in a kind and loving tone during an argument.
- Using touch to maintain connection and show care.
- Heartlead listening to empathize and understand.
- Seeing resolution as a win, rather than being right.

With a bit of care and consistency, your effective communication skills can help your romantic relationship stand the test of time. It can help you navigate struggles as a team by showing compassion and amplifying the joyous moments.

As the final chapter of this book, now is your chance to reflect back on any thoughts you have or notes you'd like to make. Go to your Workbook now and make use of the space provided.

Effective communication is a tool that's worth using – or rather dangerous to neglect. Let it improve all your important relationships as it uplifts your reputation wherever you go. With the best intentions effective communication can totally transform

SPEAK EASY

every aspect of your life. Don't be shy. Continue to apply what you've learned and stay magnetic. When you're ready, please turn the page, there's one last thing I'd like to say.

CONCLUSION

Life is beautiful. Every ounce of effort you put in to recognize that is worth it. Let your love of life and pursuit of connection carry you through to the goals you came here to achieve. And if those goals have metamorphosed under the information across these pages, honor that and keep going after what you want.

You may close this book with excitement to meet this new version of yourself – the one who was waiting for you here when you started. Welcome this version and allow it to take you over. Your life can't change if you don't. So change! Continue to be fearless in absorbing new information and being unapologetically – yet warmly – yourself.

Carry what you've learned with you, throughout this book and within the LearnWell Community, long after the exact wording has faded from your mind. And if you forget, come back to me and refresh your memory. This book is structured for easy referencing – use it. It is a resource to keep and enjoy.

Thank you for trusting me to lead you through this journey of transformation from where you were before, to exactly who you want to be. It's been a pleasure to guide you, feel with you, and sit in contemplation together. Close this final page now with pride in the shifts you were willing to make and keep up everything you've worked so hard for.

Be well and thank you.
Serina

REFERENCES

1. https://news.rice.edu/news/2006/rice-study-suggests-people-are-more-trusting-attractive-strangers
2. https://www.ncbi.nlm.nih.gov/pmc/articles/PMC8734643/
3. https://www.ncbi.nlm.nih.gov/pmc/articles/PMC2755138/
4. https://www.uaex.uada.edu/business-communities/ced-blog/posts/2022/january/most-people-think-they-are-self-aware.aspx
5. https://news.uchicago.edu/story/blind-adults-gestures-resemble-those-other-native-speakers#:~:text=New%20research%20shows%20that%20blind,make%20gestures%20in%20similar%20ways.&text=When%20people%20talk%2C%20how%20they,on%20the%20language%20they%20speak
6. https://www.health.harvard.edu/mind-and-mood/how-to-achieve-a-positive-attitude
7. https://web.archive.org/web/20140715094146/http://psych.princeton.edu/psychology/research/todorov/pdf/Willis%26Todorov-PsychScience.pdf
8. https://www.health.harvard.edu/staying-healthy/the-health-benefits-of-strong-relationships

www.ingramcontent.com/pod-product-compliance
Lightning Source LLC
Chambersburg PA
CBHW020410080526
44584CB00014B/1267